'The Other Rugby'

'The Other Rugby'

STUART SHEARD

© Stuart Sheard 2016

Published by Drop Kick Books
www.dropkickbooks.co.uk

ISBN 978-0-9567444-5-6

British Library Cataloguing in Publications Data

A catalogue record for this book is available from the British Library

Book and cover design by Clare Brayshaw

Prepared and printed by:

York Publishing Services Ltd
64 Hallfield Road
Layerthorpe
York YO31 7ZQ

Tel: 01904 431213

Website: www.yps-publishing.co.uk

In memory of Mary

Contents

Acknowledgements

Steven Beech

Phil Caplan

Evan Charlesworth

Paul Rickett

Ian Williams

With particular thanks to Darryl Osborne

I am very grateful to the Rotherham Advertiser and Sheffield Newspapers for allowing me to use the majority of the photographs and illustrations. Steven Beech, Evan Charlesworth and Ian Williams supplied the rest.

I would like to thank Daniel Sheard for proofing and editing, Paul Rickett for his excellent foreword and Clare Brayshaw for her outstanding work on the design and layout of the book.

REMEMBERING:

Harry Brooks

Glyn Chandler

Howard Charlesworth

Andrew Hallam

Foreword by Paul Rickett

Sports Editor Rotherham Advertiser

Wading through the Advertiser archives to dig out a few pictures for this worthy tome, one thing was striking...why the heck isn't there rugby league in Rotherham anymore?

The pictures, some you'll see in this book, tell the story of a vibrant club which broke down the barriers of a round-ball obsessed town, from early roots right through to the strides made in the summer game. They were fascinating to thumb through: the old black and white pictures of Bernie Hunter and a slim line Andy Tyers, up to John Dudley and Gary Woodcock knocking seven bells out of the opposition, all now shadows of local sporting history.

Watching Rotherham through their incarnations has been grassroots sport at its best. I took a photographer along to one match – his amateur RL baptism – and it was a jaw dropper for him when, as often happened, a fist flew and then 20-odd (some very odd) players became embroiled in a brawl.

One older, genteel-looking, chap on the touchline then launched into a verbal tirade against the opposition/officials/a stray dog and people passing on a bus that would have made a Docker blush. Our photographer loved it; rugby in the raw.

It was all part and parcel of a rugby league Saturday afternoon, none of that Super League mamby-pambyness, good old agricultural rugby whereby you called a spade a shovel and after the fun and frolics, everyone went off for a pint.

It's such a shame that the sport has been lost to Rotherham after so much work went into the club over 30 years or so, thanks to some sterling work behind the scenes.

What many don't realise it that any form of team sport needs a root and branch group of willing workers, washing the kit, putting the flags out, arranging matches and paying the bills. They're the people who give any club a beating heart.

Rotherham had some of the best and one instance sums that up for me. Good old Darryl Osborne used to dictate his match reports for the 'Tiser on to one of those natty little dictaphones and then send the tape on to us to be transcribed. I gave him a call back after receiving one... asking what the running water was in the background.

"Didn't have much time at work so had to do it while I nipped to the little boys' room," he said. Now that's commitment.

Hopefully one day we'll get the game back – and I just hope that Stuart's excellent book will inspire a few enthusiasts to get the ball rolling again. When it does, I'll be there.

Introduction

This book tells the story of how rugby league arrived in Rotherham, struggled, prospered, declined and finally disappeared. The book doesn't contain lists of statistics for every year. There were, I believe, some seasons that are probably best forgotten! However, if the club hadn't survived the first season there wouldn't have been a story to tell. In my opinion that first season is the most significant, and for that reason it is the only one with a full list of player appearances, scorers and games won and lost.

I have also included some statistical information about players who have been 'stalwarts,' made important contributions, or were leading scorers. However, what you won't find in the book are stories about funny incidents or the after match activities that anyone who has ever played rugby will know all about. For former players those memories will, I am sure, come flooding back when they read about the period when they were involved. 'The Other Rugby' is a story told from my experiences and observations and, of course, some people are naturally mentioned more than others. If you are a former player and can't find your name in the book I hope you can at least find your face on one of the photographs.

The first fifteen years of this story are my memories. For the period after 1992 I am very grateful to Darryl Osborne, Evan Charlesworth, Chris Bell and Paul Rickett for their recollections that have added to my knowledge of the club at that time, gleaned mainly from the Rotherham Advertiser and as an occasional spectator.

Rugby arrives in Rotherham

The Northern Rugby Football Union was formed in 1895 when twenty-two of the leading rugby union clubs in the north of England left the Rugby Football Union (RFU) to set up their own competition. In the years following the breakaway the Northern Union gradually changed the rules of the game in order to make it more interesting to spectators, in the process creating their own distinct sport which was separate from rugby union. One of the main changes was a reduction in the number of players on the field from fifteen to thirteen. By the mid-1920s the governing body had changed its name from the Northern Union to the Rugby Football League, and the game was then re-named rugby league. Despite being extremely popular in other parts of Yorkshire (and particularly in West Yorkshire), rugby league had never really taken hold in the southern part of the County. In fact, until the early 1920s neither code of rugby had any presence in Rotherham, where soccer was the dominant sport. Rotherham United FC wasn't formed until 1925 but prior to that the town had boasted two professional soccer clubs and a soccer history that went back to 1870 when Thornhill was the senior club.

The 1920s saw a big increase in the number of rugby union clubs joining the Yorkshire Rugby Football Union. This influx of new clubs has often been referred to as the 'rush to rugby'. One of the factors that contributed to the 'rush to rugby' may have been the sense of normality that the end of World War One brought. Many of the men who had returned home from the fighting in France had gone back to their normal jobs. They had a little more leisure time at the weekends, usually Saturday afternoon, and some were perhaps keen to play a sport that prior to the turn of the century had been, in the North of England, as popular as soccer. The oval ball game arrived in Rotherham in 1923, when Rotherham Rugby Union Club was formed. With the dominance that soccer had in the town, it isn't surprising that the rugby union club struggled in the 1920s and 30s to raise its profile and improve its fixture list. In those day clubs had to negotiate with potential opponents and agree fixtures. It isn't difficult to imagine that opposition fixture secretaries were possibly not easily attracted to playing a club situated in a small industrial town in the south of the County. Rotherham's steady rise to the second tier of English rugby union really began in the 1970s. As members of the RFU Championship they are now a professional club, one that relies on sponsorship, funding from the RFU, its Directors and also gate receipts to keep it afloat.

In 1977, when the story of rugby league in Rotherham begins, the rugby union club wasn't, of course, a professional outfit, but it did dominate the rugby scene in the town. Rotherham Rugby Union Club was, at the time, gradually improving its fixture list and attracting some of the better players from other local clubs. There were some rumours that the club was offering generous expenses to players to move to Rotherham, but of course they were only rumours. Perhaps players were keen to join Rotherham because the club was successful on the field and beginning to attract better quality opposition to its Clifton Lane ground. It was against this background of a town dominated by soccer and with an ambitious rugby union club that the first steps were made to establish a rugby league club in Rotherham.

Chapter 1

Forming The Club

Imoved to Rotherham in 1969 and had been living and working there for seven years. I had played both rugby union and rugby league in Leeds and when I moved to South Yorkshire I began playing for Barnsley Rugby Union Club and Bentley, an amateur rugby league club based in Doncaster, at the time the nearest club to where I lived. Bentley was a very well-run club that had, for a number of years, dominated the small amateur scene in the town. I was captain of the Sunday League side, a member of the club committee and had just been elected Secretary of the Doncaster Amateur Rugby League. The Bentley team was competitive, successful in the local cup competitions and playing on a Sunday morning meant that I could play some rugby union on the Saturday as well. However, the journey to Bentley took at least thirty minutes, longer at 'rush hour' when you were trying to get to training on time. I had thought for a while that it would be a lot easier playing for a club in the town where I lived and worked. I also thought that a town the size of Rotherham, with a similar industrial heritage to Doncaster, should be able to support an amateur rugby league club. Doncaster, only fifteen miles from Rotherham, is a town with a professional rugby league club that was formed in the 1950s and a rugby league history that goes back over ninety years. Doncaster was hardly a 'hotbed' of the sport in the 1970s but I am fairly sure that if you mentioned rugby league in Doncaster people would know what you were talking about. In Rotherham, on the other hand, people either didn't know there were two rugby codes or if they had heard of rugby league they thought it was a sport only played by professionals. However, despite the majority of people in Rotherham appearing to have little or no knowledge of rugby league, I thought that in a town with a population of over two hundred thousand there must be somebody besides myself with an interest in the sport. The problem, of course, was that finding those enthusiasts wasn't an easy task in the days before social media.

In 2016, anyone who wants to find other people with a shared interest can just use Facebook or Twitter. In the 1970s, before anyone had ever coined the phrase 'social media', I thought that probably the only way to locate rugby league enthusiasts in Rotherham was to use the local press.

Plans for other kind of rugby

Rugby League fans in Rotherham have for years been left out in the cold.

Their kind of rugby has hardly shown its face South of Doncaster, and in Rotherham and the surrounding district the only kind of rugby played is Rugby Union.

But that could change. Plans are afoot to seek out the rugby league lovers amongst us and get them together to form one of the county's new amateur clubs.

The man who hopes to bring the game to Rotherham is Stuart Sheard, a teacher, of 13, Godstone Road, Rotherham. He is secretary at Doncaster and District Amateur Rugby League Club, and he believes that there are more than enough people in the Rotherham area to form a club here.

"We are hoping to get in touch with publicans or anyone with previous connections with the game who might have moved into the Rotherham area," Mr. Sheard told "The Advertiser".

"We're pushing to expand rugby league in towns that don't already have an amateur team, and we feel that Rotherham is a town which could easily support its own club," he said.

He said that amateur rugby league could be much more popular if rugby union clubs did not ban players who were over 18 and who had played rugby league—either professionally or with an amateur club.

"I agree that professional players should be excluded but the amateur side is a different thing altogether", he said. "I think it should be everyone's free choice. A lot of players would like to turn out on Saturday to play rugby union and then on play rugby league on Sunday morning when the West Yorkshire League has its matches.

"At the moment the Rugby Football Union is solid but I don't think it will be long before there is some shift," he said.

So any rugby league fans who go along with Mr. Sheard can get in touch with him by telephoning Rotherham 66545, after school hours.

Of course, I had no idea whether anyone interested in rugby league actually bought and read the local newspaper, however it did seem to be the only option and so I decided I would try to get an article about rugby league into the Rotherham Advertiser. My theory was that if some potential players saw the article and contacted me I could suggest that they spread the word amongst their friends, and if that produced a large enough group keen to play then forming a club might be viable.

When I made the decision to try and find out whether there was any interest in the sport in Rotherham I also had a few doubts about whether it would be a good idea to leave Bentley. I thought that I was unlikely to find any experienced rugby league players living in Rotherham. Without players with some rugby league experience a new club would struggle to compete against clubs from West Yorkshire. Playing for a club that was closer to home was an attractive proposition, but I wasn't sure that I wanted to end my playing career with a new club struggling to become established. Leaving Bentley for a new club in 'alien' territory didn't seem like the smartest move I could make. I'm still not certain what finally persuaded me to leave Bentley but it definitely wasn't the initial response I got to the article about 'The Other Rugby' that appeared in the Rotherham Advertiser on Friday 14th January 1977.

The story attracted very little interest. The only person who did get in touch was Harry Brooks, a teacher of the blind who lived in Rotherham and worked in Bradford. Harry, who had a lifelong interest in rugby league, was very enthusiastic about the idea of a club in Rotherham, but as he was in his mid-fifties he certainly wasn't going to be playing. Harry offered his support but said his work commitments and daily travel to Bradford meant that it would be difficult for him to help with setting up a new club. Harry's enthusiasm was encouraging but until some people, still young enough to play, came along it was hard to imagine that it would ever be possible to get a club off the ground.

Harry Brooks presenting the end of season awards in 1986

A few weeks went by without any new contacts, but despite the apparent lack of interest I thought that it might be worth having one more attempt to locate some rugby league enthusiasts. If there was no response to a second article I decided that I would stay at Bentley, and get involved in helping the new clubs in Barnsley and Doncaster to become established.

The second Rotherham Advertiser article appeared on 18th February 1977.

HOPES ALIVE

Hopes for rugby league in Rotherham are still alive despite a truly dispiriting initial response.

Stuart Sheard, the campaigner for rugby league, was expecting a little more than one reply when he called for the "other" rugby in Rotherham.

"Barnsley got going straight away and should play their first match on March 6th," Stuart said.

"Sheffield are going strong too but there's something wrong in Rotherham.

"I'm sure that there must be people who are interested but whether they are the sort of people who don't like to come forward I don't know.

"I think the next step is to go round pubs and clubs, I'm not giving up, I'm sure we could have a team here."

Belated replies in favour of rugby league can be sent to Stuart Sheard at 13, Godstone Road, Rotherham, who can be reached by telephone at Rotherham 66545.

Much to my surprise, even though the article was shorter than the previous one and not as prominent in the sports pages, it did produce better results. A guy called Tony Lidster rang me, said he was keen to play, and had some mates who were also interested in rugby league. I then got a couple of other calls including possibly the most significant one which, to my surprise, was from an experienced rugby league player. Roger Render lived and worked in Rotherham but had played rugby league in Dewsbury and was keen to both play and coach the team. Now that I had found a few players and maybe even a coach, a rugby league club in Rotherham looked more of a possibility. The next step was to hold a meeting persuade some of the people who had contacted me to become officials and formally launch the club. I didn't want to pay for a meeting room as I wasn't sure how many people would turn up, so I decided to find a quiet pub near the town centre where a few of us could sit around and talk about what to do next. The Charter Arms, a new pub next to the market complex seemed an ideal venue. The pub had a quiet downstairs room and so on Tuesday 5th April 1977 a meeting was held there to attempt to form an amateur rugby league club in Rotherham.

Prior to that first meeting I had met up with Tony Lidster, who said he was sure that a lot of his mates would be keen to play and as well as finding players, Tony also said he was happy to be the club secretary. There were ten people at the inaugural meeting including three representatives from another local club, Sheffield Concord: Dave Clarke, Alex Jarvis and Roger Richards. Concord had been in existence for about a year and had struggled to compete with clubs from more established rugby league areas. However, the three blokes from Sheffield had some experience in organising a new club and so their presence was welcome. The other people at the meeting were Tony Lidster, Roger Render, Harry Brooks, Ted Pickering, Dave Bedford and Lindsay Jarvis. A neighbour of mine called Philip Alexander, who was a journalist, came along to take the minutes. I was there in my role as Secretary of the Doncaster Amateur Rugby League with the aim of trying to keep the meeting on track. We managed to organise some officials. Harry Brooks agreed to be Chairman, Ted Pickering Treasurer, Tony Lidster was confirmed as Secretary and after a long discussion we also decided that the club should be called Rotherham Rangers. The first training session for the new team was scheduled for Wednesday 13th April on Herringthorpe Playing Fields. It was also agreed that if some friendlies could be arranged over the summer then the club might be in a position to join the West Yorkshire Sunday League and begin to play league fixtures in September 1977. The meeting, despite the large quantity of alcohol consumed, seemed to have achieved its aims.

The formation of the new club was announced in the Advertiser and the Rotherham Star, and although the articles were small they did attract some additional interest from potential players.

The early training sessions were mainly concerned with Roger Render teaching some of the new players the basics of the sport, such as how to pass, tackle and play the ball. Attendances at these sessions were small but it was hoped that the friendlies would generate a bit more interest.

Amateur rugby league team

Rotherham now has its own Amateur Rugby League team. They are already training and hope to play a match before the end of this month.

Rotherham Rangers A.R.L.F.C. were formed in a quiet town centre pub. They now have a club committee, they held their first training session on Wednesday at Herringthorpe, and have a fixture booked against Sheffield Concord.

The only thing Rangers don't have sorted out yet is where their headquarters are to be. Officials are looking for a likely pub or working men's club to adopt them.

The club secretary, Tony Lidster, of 31, Snowden Way, Brinsworth, now faces the task of getting a regular team together, and getting some results against more established opposition to make the venture a success.

If you fancy yourself as a rugby league man why not get in touch with Tony at Rotherham 75549.

Rugby league club for Rotherham

By a staff reporter

AN amateur Rugby League club has been formed at Rotherham and it is hoped to draw up fixtures for next season.

The decision to form Rotherham Rangers was taken at a meeting of enthusiasts.

It is now hoped to begin regular Wednesday evening training sessions at Herringthorpe Stadium, Rotherham, and to have a trial match with another newly formed club, Sheffield Concord.

Mr Stuart Sheard of Doncaster, who helped to form the Rotherham club, said a committee of four has been set up to get things organised for next season.

At the inaugural meeting it was decided that the first friendly should be held in Rotherham. So, just over two weeks after being formed the first game was arranged for Sunday 24th April against Sheffield Concord. However, before that game could take place there were two major obstacles to overcome. The first was that the club had no playing kit and the second that there wasn't an obvious venue in Rotherham where a rugby league match could be played. The kit issue was fairly easy to resolve as my brother-in-law Gary Halloway played for the Leeds club Middleton Arms and his dad Ron was the club secretary. I approached Ron and asked him whether the new Rotherham club could either borrow or buy a set of old shirts. Ron managed to find fifteen shirts that had once been green and gold but were now grey and grey! Ron said Rotherham could borrow the shirts for the time being and also agreed that once the club got some money together they could buy them for £20. The problem of finding a pitch was, however, proving much more difficult to resolve. There were rugby pitches on Herringthorpe Playing Fields, but they were used by the rugby union club. When Tony Lidster enquired about hiring a pitch the initial response from the Council was that it wouldn't be possible as they were marked out for rugby union and used every Saturday by the rugby union club. It took a lot of persuasion, I think mainly by Tony, to finally get the Council to agree that Rangers could use one of the rugby pitches and that it didn't need to be marked out for rugby league. Tony got the strong impression that playing the Concord game on a rugby union pitch on Herringthorpe Playing Fields was a 'one off' and that if he asked again he wouldn't be given permission. I decided that I wasn't going to play in the game against Concord as Bentley had a fixture on that day. Rotherham lost the game but Tony Lidster reported that the players who turned out were keen for more. Further friendlies were arranged against Barnsley, Emley and a new Doncaster club called Bullcroft, but after the problems Tony had in finding a pitch in Rotherham it was decided that those games would have to be away. The second friendly at Barnsley could have been a disaster as just after half-time, with Barnsley winning 18-0, Tony Sheridan, one of the Rotherham players, broke his ankle badly and the game had to be abandoned. Fortunately, the incident didn't affect the morale of the players; Tony made a good recovery, although he didn't play again, and the rest of the players were keen for another game. The next friendly away at Bullcroft also resulted in defeat, as did the game against Emley. I hadn't played in any of the first four games, but when the final friendly was organised against a Leeds club called United Services I decided I was going to play and also strengthen the team with a few 'ringers' (players registered with other clubs). The game was played at the Buslingthorpe Vale ground in Leeds. I persuaded my brother-in-law Gary to play, he got a couple of mates from Middleton to come along and one of Roger Render's mates from Dewsbury also played. The game was the most competitive of the five, with Rangers only losing by 23-8. The Rotherham-based players knew they wouldn't have the 'ringers' in their team for future league games but they had probably learned a lot about rugby league by playing in a game with a few more experienced players. I think it might have been the game against United Services and the enthusiasm of the blokes new to rugby league that finally convinced me that I should leave Bentley and play for Rotherham. Attendances at training were still small but we did continue to attract new players, mainly through word of mouth, and so it looked as if we might have sufficient players to start the season.

It was difficult to get very much press coverage during the summer as the Advertiser was focussed on cricket and the start of the new soccer season, but we did get a photograph and article in the Sheffield Saturday evening sports paper, 'The Green Un.' This was the first photograph the club had managed to get in the local press and it did encourage a couple of potential players to turn up at the Playing Fields the following Wednesday.

Roger Render feeding the ball into a four man front row!

Chapter 2

The First League Season

The first league season was a struggle from beginning to end. It started with some optimism, mainly from the guys who hadn't played rugby league before. The few of us who had played were a bit more realistic. Just being able to say that there was a club in Rotherham playing regular fixtures was probably the most we could hope for.

We continued to train during the summer and played in a couple of seven-a-side exhibition events at sports galas in Dronfield and Sheffield. The galas didn't attract any new players but they kept the interest of the blokes who were training regularly. Newcomers appeared most weeks but some of them only trained once or twice and didn't re-appear when fixtures began. Despite never managing to have more than a dozen players at training, at any one time, it did look, from the number who said they wanted to play, that we should be able to field a team. At the beginning of September the major unresolved problem was that we were still struggling to find a pitch in Rotherham. We were told by the Council that the pitches on Herringthorpe Playing Fields were solely for rugby union and couldn't have rugby league games played on them, even on a Sunday when they weren't being used. We didn't know whether the Council was under pressure from the rugby union club not to allow this 'alien' sport to be played on what they saw as their pitches. We also wondered whether the Council saw us as some sort of 'fifth columnists' setting up a rugby league club in order to destabilise and undermine the rugby union club. We didn't know why we couldn't hire a pitch on Herringthorpe and every request we made to the Council was met with a polite no. We were getting pretty desperate when, fortunately, a couple of weeks before the first game the Education Department came to our rescue and said that we could use the pitch and changing rooms at Thomas Rotherham Sixth Form College.

Thomas Rotherham College

The three major obstacles (players, kit and a pitch) seemed to have been overcome and so we could start to plan for our first game in the West Yorkshire League, at home to Sheffield Concord on Sunday 18th September 1977. However, 'plan' is probably not the correct description for what happened prior to a game in those days. In 1977, just getting a team on the field was the number one priority and we didn't have any idea of what to do if we couldn't find at least thirteen players who wanted to play. Until eleven o'clock on the morning of the game none of us really knew whether we would have a full team. There was a preview of the first game in the Advertiser, we organised a photographer from the Sheffield Star to take a team photograph and 'crossed our fingers'.

There were eighteen players named in the preview but I am pretty sure that at least three of the names were there just to give the impression that we were selecting a team from a squad of players, rather than the reality which was that we hoped at least thirteen were going to turn up. A positive for all new clubs in the 1970s was that rugby league teams only had two substitutes rather than the four allowed today. That meant it was a little easier, in theory, to get a full complement of players to a game.

Unfortunately, Roger Render wasn't available for the first match due to work commitments, but new recruits Fred Toyne, who I played with at Bentley and persuaded to play for Rotherham, Mike McLoughlin, who had played rugby league in Bradford, and Kevin Ceaser, a former rugby union player, added some experience to the team. We managed to field thirteen players and one substitute, a remarkable achievement as twenty minutes before kick-off it looked very likely that we would have to start the game with twelve men. The two players who arrived late managed to get changed in time for the team photograph and Rotherham's first league game kicked off at 11.00am.

A number of the players who played in that first ever league game went on to be 'club stalwarts'. Ray Bramham was in his thirties when he started playing rugby league, not an ideal age to begin to play a very physical sport but Ray really took to rugby league and was the regular full back for many seasons. He made 139 appearances and scored just one try. Dave Henshaw, a very tough, durable prop forward who always gave 100% made 123 appearances. Alf Davis made 51 appearances and became the regular goal kicker.

The first league game resulted in a victory for Rangers by 33 points to 25. I scored three tries, Tony Lidster two, with the others coming

New trio for the Rangers

Rotherham Rangers Amateur Rugby League Club have three new players in their squad for the first West Yorkshire League game against Sheffield Concord, on Sunday at Thomas Rotherham College.

The three newcomers are Fred Toyne, former Bentley first team hooker, Mike McLaughlin, who played rugby league when he lived in the Bradford area, and Kevin Ceaser, a former rugby union player.

Scrum-half Alf Davis hopes to continue his excellent scoring record against Concord. In the two pre-season games against the Sheffield club he scored six tries and kicked 14 goals.

The team will be selected from: L. Jarvis, J. Abrahams, A. Lidster, R. Bramham, A. Davis, G. Packham, S. Sheard, R. Render, D. Oldroyd, F. Toyne, D. Henshaw, J. Essex, K. Ceaser, M. McLaughlin, K. Parlett, P. Mortimer, R. Oldroyd and D. Somanlik.

Rotherham Rangers 18th September 1977
Back row L-R Ted Pickering, Kevin Parlett, Mike McLoughlin,
Dave Wilmot, Dave Henshaw, Dave Lidster, Sam Mara, Kevin Ceaser,
John Essex,

Front row L-R Paul Mortimer, Fred Toyne, Jim Abrahams,
Stuart Sheard, Alf Davis, Ray Bramham

from Jim Abrahams, Kevin Ceaser, John Essex and Dave Henshaw. Paul Mortimer kicked three goals. We had the upper hand in the game but because we could only manage to convert three of our nine tries Sheffield Concord were always in contention. I am not sure how the players new to rugby league viewed the victory; most of them knew very little about the teams in our division and wouldn't have known whether the opposition was good or not. The truth was that Sheffield Concord had turned out a poor team and, although the win boosted morale, I certainly didn't think that beating Concord meant that we were going to have a successful season. After the game the players went back to the Davy Lamp pub in East Herringthorpe where John Essex, one of Rangers front rowers, was the landlord.

Starting the league campaign with a win was important. I wasn't getting carried away, but I was hopeful that the positive start meant that we would be able to get a full team and two substitutes on the pitch for future league games. Unfortunately, I was over optimistic; despite winning our second game away at Barnsley, a victory achieved with only twelve men, we didn't manage to field fifteen players until the 23rd October.

The excuses players made for missing a game were often very creative, not quite in "my dog died" category, but close. However, as we needed to keep everybody involved all the excuses were accepted and players who missed a game were encouraged to play the following week. Over that first season we only managed a full complement of players in nine of the twenty-five games. The early weeks were really tough. On 9th October, with twelve men, we lost 44-10 at home to Bullcroft. This, for me, was probably the low point of the season; we had come to expect that we might struggle for players when we played away, but to only raise twelve for a home game was very dis-spiriting. Bullcroft didn't just beat us, they physically dominated us and getting 'beaten up' on a cold Sunday morning with less than a full team certainly wasn't fun. However, despite the defeat we did get two men back the following week and although we lost at Moorends we managed to turn out fourteen players. Remarkably, the week after we played Moorends, we finally had a full team and two substitutes and it was for an away game! At the time I thought the reason we had fifteen players may have been because some of them had heard that our opponents, Doncaster Transport, were bottom of the league! We won easily, by 31-9, but were then back to fourteen men the following week in the Doncaster Cup against Rossington Hornets. The 60-10 drubbing we suffered at home to Rossington was probably one of the reasons that we could only field nine players the following week at Truck Components in Wakefield. We lost that game by 44-0, hardly surprising as it is pretty difficult to defend your line when the opposition has four players more than you. I think the referee took pity on us and only played thirty minutes each half which at least kept the score respectable. The Truck Components fixture was the low point for numbers and although we didn't often have a team and two substitutes there was only one other occasion that season when we played with less than thirteen men. That game was, unsurprisingly, at Bullcroft, where we only managed to field eleven Rotherham players, the twelfth being a 'ringer' that Roger Render had brought along. Fortunately, Bullcroft didn't know who the 'ringer' was and although we lost, it was only by 31-10.

In early 1978 we had to re-organise the off-field roles. Tony Lidster, mainly because of health issues, was struggling with the secretary's job. Ted Pickering disappeared from the scene after the first two games and so we had no treasurer for the first half of the season. We held a club meeting in February and Tony moved to be Chairman, Harry Brooks became Vice Chairman, Mike McLoughlin was elected as Treasurer and I agreed to be Secretary. The re-organisation got us through the rest of the season. During that first year we also struggled to find a base for refreshments after home matches. We decided that the Davy Lamp, in East Herringthorpe, was too far from the ground. The Belvedere, next to Thomas Rotherham College, would have been ideal but the landlord, despite the potential for increased trade, wasn't very interested and so we ended up at the Angel Hotel in the town centre. The landlord at the Angel agreed to put food on after matches, and although it was a mile or so from Thomas Rotherham there was lots of parking on a Sunday so the opposition players were usually happy to go there.

The other major issue we needed to resolve in that first season was playing kit. The 'grey and grey' shirts we bought from Middleton didn't look as if they were going to last the season. We didn't have any club funds as the match day 'subs' the players paid just about covered the cost of hiring the pitch, paying the referee and the after match food. We had very little chance of finding a kit sponsor as so few people in the town knew what rugby league was. Fortunately, local government re-organisation came to our rescue. South Yorkshire County Council was being dissolved, but before they went out of existence they needed to spend the money that was left in a small grants 'pot'. We applied for a grant, were successful, and managed to buy a new kit. This meant that we didn't look quite as scruffy as we would have if we had tried to use the Middleton kit all season.

The highlight of the second half of the season was a 41-10 demolition of Barnsley, easily our best performance. In total we managed to win seven out of twenty five games. Despite the struggle to raise a full team for the majority of our games there were some positives in that first season. A number of players who joined the club in early 1978 went on to make important contributions over future seasons. Kevin Gregory played 100 games for Rangers, scoring 41 tries and kicking 13 goals. Howard Charlesworth, who I knew from playing rugby union at Barnsley, joined in January 1978, made 103 appearances and, over his many years of involvement, contributed a great deal both on and off the field. Lewis White, who joined Rangers in March 1978, was one of the best players ever to play for the club. Lewis could certainly have played professional rugby league had he not been employed as a fireman, with his shift patterns meaning that he couldn't train regularly or commit to being available every weekend. Over a long playing career Lewis made 135 appearances and scored 78 tries.

The first season of rugby league in Rotherham could hardly have been judged as an unqualified success but at least the club was still in existence. New players had joined and we managed to win a few games. I am not sure that in 2016 many newly formed amateur clubs with Rotherham's dismal playing record would have been around for a second season but in 1977 winning didn't seem quite as important as getting fifteen players to a game. The converts to rugby league appeared to have enjoyed being part of a team sport. My view, as club secretary, was that getting a full team and two substitutes to every game was what was most important and although it was frustrating to lose, it was a major achievement to have a rugby league club in Rotherham playing regular fixtures.

Below is the list of appearances and scorers for the inaugural season

APPEARANCES AND SCORERS

Player	App	Tries	Goals
D. Henshaw	25	9	34
R. Bramham	24	–	–
S. Sheard	24	17	–
M. McLoughlin	22	8	–
D. Oldroyd	20	7	–
P. Mortimer	19	2	4
R. Oldroyd	19	15	–
A. Lidster	18	6	–
A. Davis	15	–	19
K. Gregory	15	5	3
R. Render	15	2	–
A. Sharpe	15	1	–
H. Charlesworth	11	2	–
I. Williams	11	1	–
J. Abrahams	10	6	–
K. Parlett	10	1	–
K. Ceasar	9	2	–
S. Owen	8	1	–
G. Morley	7	1	–
C. Ceasar	6	–	–
D. Lewis	5	5	–
S. Mara	5	1	–
N. Blacker	4	–	–
A. Shillito	4	–	–
D. Bedford	3	2	–

R. Ceaser	3	1	–
L. Jarvis	3	1	–
F. Toyne	3	1	–
J. Essex	2	1	–
M. Halder	2	–	–
R. Brown	1	–	–
D. Brown	1	1	–
B. Gilgoos	1	1	–
S. Oldham	1	–	–
S. Wilmott	1	–	–

LEADING SCORERS

Goals: Dave Henshaw – 34   **Tries:** Stuart Sheard – 17
Points: D. Henshaw – 95

Player of the Season 1977-1978 – Ray Bramham and
Robin Oldroyd

Most Improved Player 1977-1978 – Dave Henshaw
(The Brooks Trophy)

Clubman of the Year 1977-1978 – Stuart Sheard

Played 25 Won 7 Lost 18 Points for 416 Points against 586

You will not find Lewis White's name in the list. When Lewis first
joined the club he was concerned that if the Fire Service found out he
was playing rugby league he would be in trouble and might lose his job.
So Lewis is listed as D. Lewis, with five appearances and five tries.

Chapter 3

The Early Years

During the thirty-five years that a rugby league club existed in Rotherham, attracting new players often proved difficult. In the early years of the club (when even rugby union wasn't played in many secondary schools) any young men interested in a team sport inevitably played soccer in the thriving Rotherham Saturday and Sunday leagues. The few who wanted an opportunity to play rugby probably had no idea that there was even a sport called rugby league. In the early days when we made newspaper appeals for new players we usually only got one or two responses. More often, players appeared because they knew someone who played for the club. 'Bringing a mate' really worked for us when those mates had either played rugby before joining the club or they worked in a job where keeping fit was a requirement. Over the years rugby league in Rotherham had a number of such player supply routes. The first began when Lewis White joined and, during the 1978/79 season, realised he wasn't going to get into trouble at work for playing rugby league, so encouraged his mates from the Fire Service to try the sport. Alan France was the first fireman that Lewis brought to the club, and he was followed by Stuart Hobson, Graham Burns, and then Tony Blackburn.

None of Lewis's mates had ever played rugby league before but they were fit, tough blokes who adapted very quickly. Shift patterns meant that it was often difficult to get all of them on the pitch at the same time but they became good players. Stuart Hobson made 163 appearances for the club in a variety of positions; Graham Burns only made 42 appearances but was a good goal kicker while Tony Blackburn with 25 tries in the 1980/81 season held the tries in a season record for many years.

Stuart Hobson

The second league season was an improvement on the first. There was just one game when Rangers fielded less than thirteen players and that was at Moorends on 17th December 1978. With only twelve men the game was very one-sided and we lost by 45-14. We won seven games in 1978/79, the same number as in the previous season, but significantly one of the wins was in the semi-final of the Doncaster Continuation Cup, the competition for clubs knocked out in the first round of the Doncaster Cup. And so in 1979 we reached our first ever final, in which we played Bentley at Doncaster's Tattersfield ground and lost by 21 points to 12. Although the score was reasonably close, the reality was that we were never really in the game, Bentley's more experienced team was in control from the first whistle.

Another big improvement on the first season was that some of the new players joining the club had played rugby before. Many of these newcomers stayed with Rangers and strengthened the team. Kevin Bain was a strong-running forward who played 61 games. Paul Bates, who managed only one try in his 67 appearances at prop forward, was a club stalwart and chairman for a number of years. Andrew Tummon, who made 44 appearances before deciding to return to playing soccer, re-joined the club in the late 1990s to help with the coaching. Danny Sharpe was persuaded to join by his brother Alex and as well as making a playing contribution with 46 appearances he also treated many of the club's injured players at his physio practice in Rotherham. One player who joined Rangers in October 1978 made an immediate impact. Dave Platts was Rangers' first recruit from Rotherham Rugby Union Club and playing at stand-off or in the centre he was ideally suited to rugby league. However, when the hierarchy at the rugby union club found out that Dave was playing rugby league he was told that if he continued to do so he would no longer be welcome in the Clifton Lane clubhouse. Dave initially ignored the threats but the pressure built up and so after nine games, in which he scored seven tries and kicked thirteen goals, he decided to stop playing rugby league; the threats had worked. Dave thought that if he wasn't allowed in the clubhouse he would lose contact with a lot of his mates and wasn't prepared to take that risk. No other Rotherham Rugby Union Club players tried their hand at rugby league during the early years. What had happened to Dave Platts must have persuaded a few other potential recruits that if they wanted to remain welcome in the rugby union club's bar they had better not play rugby league.

Another very significant improvement that season came in November 1978 when Rangers moved from Thomas Rotherham College to the Rotherham Co-op Sports Club on Wickersley Road, a mile or so from the town centre. The problem of where to go for after-match refreshments hadn't really been resolved by the move to the Angel. The landlord was interested in the extra business but didn't really want to help the club, and the after-match food was expensive. Very few of the players went into the pub during the week and because he wasn't getting very much extra trade the landlord wasn't willing to reduce the cost of the food. The move to the Co-op Club came about because on the 9th September Rangers were drawn at home to Emley in the BARLA Yorkshire Cup. The Cup game had to be played on a Saturday afternoon but, in the days before all-day opening, finding a pub that would open at 4.30 to serve food proved impossible. The Co-op, because it was a members club, was able to open early and so we went there after the game. The Co-op Club had a cricket pitch and a football pitch on site and while it didn't seem likely that we would be able to share the football pitch, a rugby pitch on the cricket outfield did seem a possibility. After protracted discussions with the club secretary it was agreed that we could use the cricket outfield, but we needed to find some posts. We didn't have sufficient funds to buy posts and the Council said that they couldn't loan us a set but fortunately Ian Williams, who had joined the club the previous season, came up with a solution. Ian had contacts at Croda Chemicals in Mexborough and managed to acquire some steel pipes that were made into posts. The steel pipes were very heavy and it took a team effort to dig the holes and erect them. We finally managed to get everything in place so that we could play our first home game at the Co-op on Sunday 12th November 1978, against Bentley. The pitch was very small and, while it suited us at home, it was often difficult to adjust to playing on larger pitches when we played away.

Action from a game at the Co-op Club

The big bonus when we played at the Co-op was that the changing rooms and bar were next to the pitch and initially the Co-op Club committee welcomed the extra Sunday lunchtime business. There were a few Sunday regulars who grumbled about the noisy rugby players but as there weren't many of them it wasn't, to begin with, a big problem. However, after the first month or so I started to receive phone calls from

Oscar Hargreaves, the Co-op Club secretary, complaining about mess in the changing room, half naked players walking back from the showers or singing in the bar after matches. The situation wasn't easy to manage and I think it was only because of the increase in bar income that the Co-op committee allowed us to stay. The complaints unfortunately did continue and it became increasingly difficult to think up excuses or find different ways of apologising. However, we tried to keep things under control as we recognised that the Co-op gave us a proper base and although the pitch was small it was well maintained and we could use it whenever we wanted.

The next two seasons didn't see a great improvement in results but for the majority of games we were managing to turn out a team and two substitutes.

1981 Team

By this time I wasn't playing regularly, if we had fifteen players I was usually happy to watch. My commitments at the club and as Secretary of both the Doncaster and West Yorkshire Leagues meant that I had very little time to fit in training. We tried to pick the team based on who had trained and so I usually ended up as sixteenth man.

In April 1981 we made our second appearance in the Doncaster Continuation Cup Final. Tony Blackburn was playing regularly at stand-off and scoring tries most weeks but unfortunately at the end of March Tony broke his ankle. This was an injury that ended his rugby league career, ruled him out of playing in the final and meant that we were going into the game without our best player. Our opponents in the Cup Final held at Doncaster's Tattersfield ground was once again Bentley, a club we had never managed to beat. We were very competitive in the match but without Tony we struggled to score tries, wasted a lot of opportunities and lost by 15points to 10.

Doncaster Continuation Cup Final team

Although the Continuation Cup Final was probably the highlight of the season, the most significant event and one that had a major impact on the future playing strength of the club had taken place two weeks before the Cup Final. On Thursday 16th April 1981, Rangers played a friendly against Retford at the Co-op Club. Included in the Rangers team were Jon Cook at full back and Bernie Hunter at centre. Both Jon and Bernie were in their final year at Sheffield University. They were experienced players from Widnes who had been part of the rugby league

Bernie Hunter

team at the University and were planning to stay in the area when they graduated. Jon and Bernie became important members of the club and because of their involvement with Rotherham a second source of new players opened up.

For the next ten years any rugby league playing students who graduated from Sheffield University and remained in the area were persuaded by Bernie and Jon to join Rangers. Bernie made 250 appearances for the club and Jon 157. There were many quality players who joined Rangers from Sheffield University and the student connection was one of the major reasons why the club began to be much more successful on the field and make progress through the leagues.

For the next few seasons, as Rangers results improved, new players from South Yorkshire continued to appear. Chris Woodhouse who made 107 appearances and John Ambler, who made 111 appearances, played a few games for Doncaster Rugby League Club and was a prolific try scorer, were two important recruits. Andrew Tyers, a significant figure in the story of rugby league in Rotherham, was another. Andrew joined the club

Jon Cook and Andrew Tyers

as a 'slim' eighteen year old goal kicking centre after he responded to an article in the Sheffield Star suggesting that Stocksbridge, where he lived at the time, would be a good place to start a new rugby league club. The Stocksbridge club never appeared but Andrew began a playing career with Rangers that lasted over twenty years and ended with him as a far from slim prop-forward sized stand-off. He made over 200 appearances in several spells at the club as well as playing professional rugby league for Doncaster, Sheffield Eagles and Keighley. Andrew was also club coach for a number of seasons and in later years was responsible for recruiting Jordan James, the club's only Super League player.

By the early 1980s the days of Rangers turning up to games with less than a full team appeared to be long gone. However for some away games the telephone box near our meeting point in Rotherham was a lifeline. Before mobile phones were invented it was always necessary to have a pocket full of change in order to ring anybody who hadn't turned up, and dragging players out of bed on a Sunday morning was a fairly regular occurrence. We often set off to an away game with less than a full team and picked players up on the way. After the frantic phone calls to get a team together the journey was the next obstacle to overcome. We couldn't afford to hire a coach for away games and so cars' travelling in convoy was, in the days before satellite navigation, the only way we ensured that we got all fifteen players to the game. Usually only the lead car in the convoy had directions to the ground and so it was crucial if you were driving the lead car that you didn't lose anyone. If you lost a car then it usually meant starting the game four players short. Unfortunately, losing a car on the M1 seemed to become a regular occurrence. The car we lost was often driven by a player who wanted to impress his mates with his driving skills and so as soon as we got to the motorway he would race away, leaving the rest of the convoy behind. When that happened we had to hope that the driver realised before we all left the motorway that he probably didn't know which turn-off to take. Getting a team together and travelling to an away game on a Sunday morning wasn't much fun and there were times when I thought that I could find better things to do with my time. However, the trauma of finding fifteen players followed by the journey to the game was worthwhile if we beat a strong West Yorkshire club.

Rangers continued to recruit players locally and from the University and during the 1980s results steadily improved and the club consolidated its position as one of the stronger South Yorkshire outfits. In September 1982, after nearly four years playing at the Co-op Club, Rangers moved to Herringthorpe Playing Fields. This was a ground we had been desperate to use in 1977, but perhaps an indication of how far the club had come was the fact that in many respects moving to Herringthorpe was now a backward step. The Pavilion on the Playing Fields was pretty run down, the showers often didn't work and for after-match refreshments the players had to drive to the Rotherham Railway club, about half a mile away. However a move away from the Co-op Club had always seemed likely sooner or later, particularly as the volume of complaints increased. Most of the issues were really trivial but it was getting to the point when we knew we were going to be told to leave and so we decided to 'jump before we were pushed'. The Council was by now much more sympathetic to the idea of rugby league being played in Rotherham and agreed to mark out a rugby league pitch close to the Pavilion. The pitch was larger than the one at the Co-op Club and we thought this would help the players to adjust to playing on a bigger pitch both at home and away.

We did hope that the move to Herringthorpe was going to be a temporary solution and so over the next few years the search for a new home ground continued. Whenever I found a patch of grass or a farmer's field near Rotherham that looked large enough to accommodate a rugby pitch I attempted to track down the owner and see whether there was a possibility of using it. Every enquiry I made received the same negative response. I continued to talk to the Council, who were sympathetic and appeared to want to help but didn't really have any available sites. I tried a couple of sports clubs with unused soccer pitches but they weren't interested in sharing their facilities with a rugby league club. Would things have turned out differently if one of the potential new grounds had been available? I don't think playing for as long as we did on Herringthorpe Playing Fields really helped the club become firmly established but it appeared that, at the time, that there wasn't any other option.

Chapter 4

Expansion

By the mid-1980s, with results continuing to improve, the profile of rugby league in Rotherham was now generating much more interest from potential players and sponsors and there was even a second club in the town, called "Sheffield and Kimberworth". This 'new' organisation was in fact a Sheffield club that because of ground issues in Sheffield had moved to play home games at Wingfield School in the Kimberworth district of Rotherham. The club didn't stay very long in Kimberworth. After a season or so they moved back to play in Sheffield and dropped the Kimberworth part of their name.

1985 Team

There were more people in Rotherham who were now aware that the town had a rugby league club and so the occasional newspaper request for new players usually produced a much more positive response than had been the case in the 1970s. In the mid-1980s another player supply route had also opened up. Bernie Hunter began his teaching career at Clowne School, in North Derbyshire, where he started to organise rugby league coaching sessions that eventually led to the formation of an under 16 team. When the Clowne players Bernie had introduced to rugby league left school he encouraged them to join Rangers. Vinnie Waller, Adrian Taylor, Shane Higgins and Matthew Root were some of the first to join, all talented young players who had been well coached. They improved the team and in 1985 the club managed to win its first trophy, the Doncaster Continuation Cup at the third time of asking. The final against Selby was once again held at Tattersfield and was very one-sided, Rangers winning by 52 points to 4.

Continuation Cup winners

The 1985/86 season began with Rangers playing in Division 3 of the West Yorkshire League. The fact that recruiting had become easier did unfortunately have a negative effect as there were a number of players training regularly and not getting an opportunity to play. We didn't want to lose those players and so plans were made to form a second team. The idea was that the new team would play friendlies initially, with the hope of attracting further additional players that would make it possible for the 'A' team to join a League in September 1986. Articles in the Advertiser and the Rotherham Star announcing the formation of the second team attracted a number of new recruits. These included Steven Beech who, as a player and administrator, stayed with the club for over twenty five years. Anyone who ever played in the same team as Steve will, I am sure, remember his 'war cry' as he charged into the thick of the action. Darryl Osborne also joined the club as a result of the newspaper articles and he would go on to make a massive contribution to rugby league in Rotherham both on and off the field. Darryl began as a player, making over 130 appearances and kicking in excess of 280 goals. After he retired from playing Darryl became first team coach, then Director of Rugby and was the driving force behind the club's re-incarnation in the 1990s. Darryl's contribution cannot be overestimated in the story of rugby league in Rotherham. The Hawkins brothers, Nigel and Mark, also joined at the same time, and Nigel went on to make over 120 appearances as well as being first team captain for a number of years.

The 'A' team in 1985/86

In 1985/86, the first season that the club organised a second team, ten games were played, with four wins and six losses. The 'A' team matches took place on a Saturday afternoon as the reality was we didn't really have sufficient players for both teams to play on the same day, and the second team's numbers were often made up by first team players who then played again on the Sunday morning.

The 1985/86 season saw the first team finish second in division three of the West Yorkshire League, which resulted in another promotion. Hopes were high going into the tenth season of rugby league in Rotherham. Players from Sheffield University continued to join the club and Bernie Hunter's work at Clowne School resulted in a continuous supply of good young players from North Derbyshire.

The 1986/87 season began with success for the 'A' team and a slow start by the first team. The 'A' team had joined the Mansfield and Nottinghamshire League, hoping for more regular fixtures. Unfortunately joining the League didn't result in any extra fixtures as due to a lack of teams and many postponements only ten games were played. However, the bright spot was an early success when the 'A' team won a pre-season 13-a-side competition held at Nottingham Trent University. Rangers 'A' team beat a club from Mansfield called Garibaldi 14-0 in the final. Unfortunately, after that early season high-point things went rapidly downhill with the lack of regular fixtures impacting on player recruitment and retention. The 'A' team only won two of the ten games played and had to rely heavily on the first team players who 'doubled up'. Having first teamers available on some weeks and not others meant the number of players that turned out in 'A' team games varied between ten and eighteen. The involvement of first team players also caused friction as some of the 'A' team regulars were demoted to the bench if a first teamer was available in their position.

The slow start made by the first team meant that, although results picked up as the season progressed, they only managed to finish in fourth place in division two. The higher standard of rugby the first team was playing was also starting to have a negative impact. In the early days you could drag players out of bed to play knowing that the opposition had probably done the same with some of their team. In the 1970s most of the clubs we were playing against had players who were new to the game and others who were recovering from a heavy drinking session. The number of fit and experienced players in the opposition team was usually very similar to the number Rangers had. However in the mid-1980s interest in Sunday morning rugby league was declining and some of West Yorkshire League's Premier division clubs had moved to the Yorkshire League so that they could play fixtures on Saturdays. The loss of these clubs caused the League to re-organise and promote Rangers to division one, meaning that the number of good players in the opposition teams increased dramatically.

The higher standard of rugby meant that all the players knew they were in for a tough morning and so if they got a last minute call to play they were often very reluctant to turn out. The away games were usually against strong clubs in Wakefield or Castleford and very few 'A' team players, who had played the day before, were keen to play two games in the weekend, particularly if the second game was against one of the top West Yorkshire outfits. I think we first began to discuss whether it was sensible to continue playing Sunday morning rugby after the first team played against Manor in February 1988 and lost to the Wakefield-based club by 24 points to 8. For this game we had turned out what appeared on paper to be a decent team but, because quite a few of our players were still recovering from a heavy drinking session the night before, we were easily beaten. It had been a real struggle to get a team and two substitutes to the game and obviously a few of the blokes who turned out weren't really fit to play. We decided that we weren't going to be able to compete against the leading teams in the Sunday league if some of our better players were playing with hangovers or didn't want to play away because they hadn't had time to recover from a Saturday night out. As an amateur club we had to recognise that there wasn't any way to control the drinking habits of our players. So, following a discussion with some of the senior players a decision was taken to move the first team into the Yorkshire League and at the same time move the 'A' team into the Sunday League. This was an attempt to address both the problems caused by playing in the higher divisions of the West Yorkshire League and also the lack of regular 'A' team fixtures.

Two other major developments also took place in 1988. The first one was the formation of an under 17s team. Howard Charlesworth organised and coached the team and was able to recruit players from a recently formed Rotherham Schools under16 team. The Schools team had been set up following coaching sessions at several Rotherham Secondary schools led by the Sheffield Eagles development staff. The Rotherham Schools team played a few fixtures and wasn't very successful but a number of the boys who took part in the games did look to have the potential to develop into good rugby league players.

The first Under 17 training session

Howard's sons Adam and Evan both played with the under 17s team and then with the open age team in later years. Adam went on to play professional rugby league with Hull Kingston Rovers whilst Evan played for Wakefield Trinity Colts and amateur clubs in Wakefield before becoming involved again at Rotherham in 2007. Howard had been able to find sponsors to cover travel and equipment costs for the junior team, but as the year wore on finding new players became the biggest problem. Only the inclusion of some boys from Hoyland enabled the team to finish the season. Howard, after all the work he put into the under 17 team, desperately wanted it to be more than a 'one-season wonder'. However the difficulty he had in recruiting new players with some rugby experience meant a second season was never really a possibility. Fortunately there was a small group of Rotherham-based players who had managed to see out the under 17 season and were keen to stay involved in the sport. Adam and Evan Charlesworth, Mat Bownes, Steve Spruyt, Danny McLoughlin and Craig Weston all moved up to play for Rangers open age teams, with Craig later going on to become a mainstay of the club both as a player and a coach.

Under 17 team

Unfortunately, after the initial burst of enthusiasm, very few Secondary Schools had continued to play any fixtures. The Rotherham Schools team folded and by the end of the 1980s there were only one or two schools in Rotherham still playing rugby league. Sheffield Eagles' development priorities had changed and the Community coaching team was no longer interested in promoting rugby league in Rotherham schools. In 1990, without the support from Sheffield Eagles, the sport at Secondary School level fizzled out. This meant that a potential source of local players disappeared completely. Rugby league continued to be played in a few Rotherham Primary Schools in the early 1990s, but as there wasn't a pathway for these young players to continue their involvement in rugby league either at school or club level, any enthusiasm they had for the sport was lost when they entered Secondary School. Even in established rugby league towns, inter-school fixtures were declining in number and the young player who learned the game at school and then moved on to playing for an amateur club was becoming a rarity. Amateur clubs that organised junior teams were fast becoming the only places where boys could be introduced to rugby league and Rotherham Rangers unfortunately didn't have enough people with either the interest or experience required in order to set up junior teams.

A second development in 1988 was the move of club headquarters to the Cranworth Hotel on Fitzwilliam Road. Rotherham Railway Club, which had been the headquarters for four years, was never the most welcoming place. Rangers were really only tolerated because they brought income into a club that had very few regular customers. The new landlord at the Cranworth had played amateur rugby league for Askern, at the time one of the strongest clubs in Doncaster, and when we heard that he was interested in Rangers using his pub as a base we went to see him. When the move was agreed the landlord converted an outbuilding into a small dressing room with showers that we could use to get changed for training. I guess he hoped that, because they were changing in a room next to the pub, the players would call in for a pint before heading home. The changing room became a bit of a health hazard as nobody took responsibility for cleaning the showers. Also, the room was so small that once the showers were being used it very quickly filled up with steam, which made it very difficult to see who was actually in there and it also meant that everyone left the building with damp clothes.

Having the dressing room at the Cranworth did mean that pre-season and early season training could take place on Eldon Road Playing

Fields, only a two minute walk away. We explored the idea of playing home games on Eldon Road but unfortunately, with only one dressing room, using the pub for changing wasn't a possibility. Clifton School had some changing rooms on Eldon Road but they wouldn't allow us use them. The Cranworth was an ideal base to begin with, but eventually issues around the cost of food and the number of players staying for a pint after games and training soured the relationship. After a couple of years at the Cranworth it was decided to move to Rotherham Cricket Club for after match refreshments. This was a decision that would unfortunately create a major split in the club. The Cricket Club didn't open on Sunday lunchtime and so the 'A' team had to find its own base, which became a pub in Dalton called the Red Lion. The fact that the club now had two bases caused real problems for both teams. The Red Lion had a good atmosphere after games and it was understandable that the 'A' team players didn't want to lose that by playing on a Saturday for the first team. As a result, players became very reluctant to move from the 'A' team to the first team. At the end of the 1980s the 'A' team's results also began to improve and the excellent team spirit was epitomised by one remarkable victory with only ten players over a Castleford-based club called The Woodman. The 'A' team officials also began organising an end of season tour. The first 'A' team tour took place in April 1990 when a group travelled to Holland to play a game against a newly-formed Dutch team. The tours, which became annual events, were seen by the 'A' teamers as the high-point of the season. The opportunity to take part in the end of season tour was another reason why players were reluctant to swap the excellent team spirit in the 'A' team for a very tough Saturday afternoon game where perhaps they felt there wasn't the same camaraderie. In 1989 Rangers had appeared to be a progressive amateur rugby league club. Young players from South Yorkshire continued to join and the future of rugby league in the town seemed assured. However, the decision to leave the Cranworth began a slow decline, one that perhaps none of us at the time recognised. In addition to the problems caused by moving from the Cranworth there were also other issues that arose in 1990 which certainly accelerated the decline and led to the problems that finally occurred in 1991.

A 1989 Team

Chapter 5

Struggle and Merger

The split in the club that began when the first team moved from the Cranworth to Rotherham Town Cricket Club continued to widen as the defeats for the first team piled up. When the decision was first taken to move to the Yorkshire League the first team had been competitive, and the addition of four new players from the defunct High Green club had seemed to bode well for the future.

1st team 1990

It was a combination of injuries to key players, terrible fixture planning by the League (which often resulted in long runs of consecutive away games), the failure of the League to properly deal with violent and unsportsmanlike behaviour from certain opposition teams and one particular game away at Middleton that really made what began as a slow decline into a rapid one. The game at Middleton was significant because of the level of on-field thuggery and violence from the home team. There were many off-the-ball incidents resulting in injuries to Rotherham players. The touch judge, a qualified referee, saw most of the incidents but chose to ignore them. The Middleton supporters and coaching staff added to the intimidating atmosphere, and following the game three regular players decided to stop playing. We made a strong case at the disciplinary hearing for action to be taken against clubs that behaved like Middleton but the disciplinary committee wasn't interested in listening to our argument. After what had happened at Middleton and the amount of violence and thuggery in some Yorkshire League games it was understandable that nobody playing regularly in the 'A' team was keen to replace the players that had left. It seemed ironic at the time that the Middleton club that helped Rangers in 1977 should have such a negative impact in 1991. Rangers' first team finished second from bottom of the Yorkshire League fourth division that year.

The 'A' team had a much more successful season, finishing sixth in division three of the West Yorkshire League. They also organised another successful Easter tour, this time to Plymouth.

The 'A' team in 1991

The 1991/92 season saw the end of Rotherham's involvement in the Yorkshire League. The first team made a poor start to the season and morale was very low. After the problems of the previous season, fulfilling fixtures (particularly away) was proving very difficult. When the League released a new batch of fixtures in November that gave the team six consecutive away games I thought that was a recipe for disaster. I had left the club in September 1991 but when I saw the new fixture list I wrote to the Yorkshire League and asked them to consider re-arranging some of the games so that Rangers could at least play one or two at home. I told the League Secretary that if the team, which was already struggling for players, didn't have a home game for six weeks it could well fold. Unfortunately my request was ignored; the League wasn't prepared to make any fixture changes. The League officials, it seemed, weren't too concerned about losing Rotherham Rangers and gave the impression that they were more interested in the fines the club would have to pay if the first team dropped out of the League. Rangers withdrew from the Yorkshire League in December 1991 and the 'A' team was left to pick up the pieces. Many former first team regulars left the club. Some retired from the game; Bernie Hunter began refereeing,

The South West Yorkshire XIII that played a Sheffield Eagles team in the first rugby league game played at the Maltby Miners Welfare ground.

Matthew Root (a prolific point scorer) and Keith Ridgeway, who was coaching the team, joined Sheffield Tigers Rugby Union Club. A few of the Derbyshire and Sheffield-based players went to play for the club in Clowne while one or two of the players who lived in Rotherham joined Maltby, a new Rotherham-area team which appeared on the scene in 1991. This new club was based at the Miners Welfare ground, with good facilities and excellent financial support from the Miners Welfare Club. Maltby made a good start to the 1991/92 season and it seemed likely, given the problems Rangers were facing in 1991 that they would soon become the strongest club in the area.

Left effectively as a standalone entity in the West Yorkshire League, the 'A' team's strength built around team spirit and camaraderie was really tested and it was that spirit that got the club through a very difficult situation. There were financial issues and fines resulting from the first team's withdrawal from the Yorkshire League as well as the problem of organising the club's activities and ultimately deciding whether it was possible for Rotherham Rangers to continue. Darryl Osborne and Kevan Cadman managed to keep the club going through a very dark period, with no club funds and, as you can see from the team photo, a severe shortage of kit.

A 1992 Team

● Rotherham Rangers: Pictured from left (front): Craig Weston, Charlie Brooks, Kev Cadman, landlord of the Dene Brook Mick Mangham, Darryl Osborne, Paul Hibbert and physio Amanda Chapman. Back: Mick Fry, George Waslidge, Steven Beech, Phil Hind, Angus Wright, Dave Lidster, Mick Haig and Andy Palmer.

New sponsored kit

Having stalwarts like Angus Wright, George Waslidge, Nick Fry and Dave Lidster involved was crucial as Darryl and Kevan attempted to keep the club afloat. Dave Lidster was an inspiring leader on the field, made over 200 appearances and was team captain for eight seasons. Mick Mangham, the landlord of the Red Lion, moved to a pub called the Dene Brook and the team moved with him. Mick supported the club financially and provided the after match food which meant that, despite a string of poor results, the team was able to get through the season.

A revival on horizon for Rangers?

ROTHERHAM RANGERS are this weekend hoping to announce a move which should give a hefty upswing to rugby league in the town.

RUGBY LEAGUE

Rangers' fortunes have dwindled in recent years, the Saturday team which played at Yorkshire League level having practically disbanded while the Sunday team have struggled in the Bass West Yorkshire Division Two.

But now Rangers are formulating a plan which they hope will inject new life into the club.

Meanwhile, Rangers are on their travels this Easter, spreading the word to the north east, where Rugby League is gradually gaining a foothold.

Rotherham will play Gateshead on April 10 at Gateshead International Stadium followed by a match against Sunderland on the April 11.

Rangers are back in action this weekend after being without a match last Sunday.

They travel to take on Fox Inn of Barnsley in a West Yorkshire League match and hope to field a stronger side after successive weeks of depletion due to injury.

Eddie Willey and Mick Haigh look set to return, while Matt Green is back in the side after a three-season lay off following a badly broken leg.

Squad (meet Herringthorpe 9.30): Beresford, Waslidge, Willey, Toothill, Wright, Osborne, Weston, Green, Palmer, Cadman, Haigh, Hind, Tyers, Fry, Lidster, Faraday, Beech.

Darryl and Kevan found it very difficult to find the funds to pay the Yorkshire League fines and recover from the problems caused when the first team folded. The other major difficulty they had was finding ways to recruit players who would make the team more competitive. Any new players who joined had to be encouraged to 'buy in' to the team spirit and camaraderie and fortunately most of the new recruits did. Although results in the West Yorkshire League continued to be disappointing, at least the club was fulfilling fixtures and building a good team spirit. The end of season tours, unusual for such a small amateur rugby league club, had a massive impact on the morale of the players and officials.

A significant development occurred when a new junior club appeared on the scene in 1992. The enthusiasts behind the club, mostly Sheffield Eagles supporters, wanted the new club, which they originally called Wickersley, to provide opportunities for young people from the Rotherham area to become involved in junior rugby league.

The first game for the new Wickersley club

The club initially hoped to organise teams in the under 10, under 12 and under 14 age groups, recruit more coaches and provide an opportunity for young people up to the age of eighteen to become involved in rugby league. Shortly after being formed the new club began playing home games at the Pitches Sports Club, previously the Co-op Club, and changed their name from Wickersley to Rotherham Rams.

Meanwhile, Rangers were continuing to re-build but it was a very slow process and results were still disappointing. With more successful clubs in Sheffield and Maltby to compete with it was obviously going to take time to persuade players to move to a struggling club that, at the time, didn't seem to have much of a future.

After another year of disappointing results, Darryl and Kevan decided that the only way forward for Rotherham Rangers was a merger with Rotherham Rams. They saw the merger as an opportunity to strengthen the off-field administration, provide the open age club with a new home ground and a junior structure that would, in time, produce future players. Open age rugby league in Rotherham had, as was the case in many similar sized clubs, always been organised by the players. One or two non-players had become involved, including a guy called Andrew Duckering who helped to organise the 'A' team's activities in the late 1980s and was involved in setting up the first tour. Andrew left the club after a couple of seasons and in the fifteen years that the club had been in existence he was probably the only non-player apart from Harry Brooks in the late 1970s who had made a significant contribution.

The benefit for the junior club from a merger seemed to be the opportunity to be part of a pathway that would allow the young players produced by the Rams to have a playing opportunity in Rotherham when they reached open age level. The suggestion of a merger initially received a lukewarm reception with resistance from people involved with both clubs. However, Darryl and Kevan continued to meet with the Rams officials and eventually in 1993, with a few dissenters on both sides, an agreement was reached. The new club was called Rotherham Amateur Rugby League Club with a playing base at Pitches Sports Club, three junior teams and one open age team. The club colours were changed to red, white and blue, work was undertaken on the changing rooms at Pitches and the new club was launched.

The merger began a period of sustained growth for rugby league in Rotherham and was certainly the catalyst for the success that the club would go on to achieve in the late 1990s. It is interesting to speculate on the direction rugby league in Rotherham might have taken if Rotherham Rams had been formed five years earlier. Howard Charlesworth's under 17 team may well have continued if there had been a group of under 16 players that could have moved up. If rugby league was going to become a permanent feature of the sporting scene in the town, then providing the open age team with local players who had some experience of rugby league was obviously going to be crucial to achieving that objective.

Chapter 6

Rotherham Amateur Rugby League Club

The merger and move to Pitches Sports Club signalled the beginning of a real revival at open age level. The Rams officials Ian Oxley, Tony Hickey and Pete Moore added a great deal of organisational experience and the club had, for the first time, a proper working committee that wasn't just made up of players. The link up with Rotherham Rams also enabled young players like Rob North, Sam Moore and Nicky Colley to progress smoothly from junior to open age rugby. At the same time the rugby league club in Maltby, after a promising start, had struggled to become established and problems began to emerge off the field. The main one being friction between the rugby league club and the Miners Welfare club. The off-field problems and relative lack of success resulted in players like the Hutton brothers, Dave Williams and Steve Ridyard moving to Rotherham.

The start of the 1994/95 season saw more changes. Darryl Osborne, after injury and illness, had to retire from playing; he decided to take his coaching badge and began coaching the open age team. New players continued to join, results gradually improved and for the first time since the problems of the early 1990s Rotherham reached a local cup final. The influx of players continued with a group of experienced men arriving from Sheffield including Nigel Short, Russ Nelson and Glyn Chandler. The most significant change, however, was the decision to once again move from Sunday morning rugby league in the West Yorkshire League to Saturday afternoon rugby, this time in the Pennine League. This decision started the club on an upward trajectory of success, something that didn't happen in the 1980s when the club moved to the Yorkshire League. If Rangers had been allowed to join the Pennine League in the 1980s then perhaps some of the problems in the early 1990s might have been avoided, but the regional league at the time wasn't admitting teams from South Yorkshire. However, in the mid-1990s with the Yorkshire League in terminal decline, the Pennine League did begin to pick up the slack and admit teams from South Yorkshire, allowing Rotherham to join. The Pennine League, which at the time had seven divisions, provided a much more even standard of competition. This league was also much tougher on clubs with poor disciplinary records and as a result the discipline issues that ultimately caused the demise of the Yorkshire League were not a major issue.

The end of season tours continued, with Scotland the destination in 1995. The junior section was thriving and the future for rugby league in Rotherham appeared to be very bright. The open age club had, for the first time ever, a proper junior structure that was expected to ensure a continuous supply of young players with rugby league experience. The emphasis Darryl and Kevan placed on recruiting locally-based players and fostering a good team spirit was certainly beginning to produce results. Unfortunately, just as the club was starting to make progress both on and off the field, issues arose at Pitches Sports Club that forced the committee to look for yet another home ground. The move this time was to Ravenfield Sports Ground, four miles from Rotherham, where, unfortunately, the facilities were not as good as at Pitches. The location of Pitches, close to the town centre, plus the on-site social facilities made it a welcoming venue for rugby league at both open age and junior level. With hindsight it is possible to suggest that the move away from Pitches, with its child and parent-friendly facilities, did have a detrimental effect on junior recruitment and ultimately the slow decline of the junior section. The reasons why the club left Pitches are not clear but the Rotherham club committee felt at the time that they had no alternative. The move to Ravenfield, although it had an adverse effect on junior recruitment, didn't appear to create any problems for the open age players. The team was in division six of the Pennine League, where the standard of rugby was much better than in the West Yorkshire League. The good results on the field encouraged even more players to join, allowing the club to return to fielding two teams. However, unlike the early days of the second team in the 1980s there were now sufficient players for two teams to be able to play on the same day. What Darryl and the club committee had achieved in the mid-1990s represented great progress for rugby league in Rotherham.

Success in the 1990s

The club remained at Ravenfield for two seasons before moving again, this time closer to the centre of Rotherham with a pitch on Scrooby Lane at Parkgate. The pitch at Parkgate was the sixth home ground (including two separate stays at Pitches Sports Club) in the twenty years the club had been in existence. The facilities at Parkgate were very basic and the players had a five minute walk from the changing rooms to the pitch, but despite the poor facilities the success continued. The first team was winning regularly and the players were adapting well to the higher standard of rugby.

Unfortunately, the move to Parkgate didn't help the junior section. Two moves of home ground in four years certainly had a detrimental effect on the junior teams. Recruitment slowed and the junior section began to struggle to field competitive teams. New open age players continued to join but perhaps the long-term future was not as assured as appeared to be the case when the junior and senior clubs merged in 1993. Following the move to Parkgate, the club headquarters became the Fitzwilliam Hotel and the changing rooms were temporary buildings in the car park. Ron Hull, the owner of the pub, had promised the club that he would develop the Scrooby Lane ground by adding changing rooms and floodlights, but that plan never came to fruition. The club remained at Parkgate for two seasons before another move, this time back to Thomas Rotherham College. However, the pitch that Rangers had previously played on in front of the College was no longer used for rugby and unfortunately after just one game on a pitch behind the College the club was told to move next door and use the rugby pitch at Oakwood School. However, one positive from the move was that Mick Mangham had recently taken over the Belvedere pub and so the club was able to base itself there. Mick, who had sponsored the club since 1990, was much more supportive than the guy who ran the Belvedere in 1977 when Rangers had previously played at Thomas Rotherham College.

Another successful season

Despite the third move of home ground in five years the open-age teams continued to be successful. Darryl, who by now had moved from first team coach to Director of Rugby, continued to actively recruit new players. The first team was made up entirely of locally based men, with a number of them having made the successful transition from junior rugby. Back-to back promotions meant that, by the end of the decade, the 1st team was playing in Pennine League division one.

Rotherham Rugby League Club was now successful at a level that could only have been dreamed about in 1977. What Darryl and the enthusiasts he recruited during the 1990s had achieved was remarkable. I have little doubt that when clubs in more established rugby league areas saw they had an away fixture against

ROTHERHAM made it four straight Pennine League promotions after rounding off the season in style with a 23-12 victory at rivals Emley Moor.

It was a superb performance against a side also chasing a Pennine League first division slot next season.

They were forced into making several changes. Scott North came in after some impressive performances for the Alliance team, along with youngster Dave Harrison. Mick Chadwick moved to stand off and Chris Jasinski moved into the pack.

Rotherham then they would travel to South Yorkshire with a certain amount of trepidation. By the year 2000 Rotherham had a big pack of tough and uncompromising forwards who set a platform for a free-scoring back line. They were a team that intimidated opponents but could also play good rugby.

Back to back promotions

If the 1999/2000 season was a 'high point' for open age rugby league in Rotherham, what happened over the next two years had the potential to really put Rotherham Rugby League Club on the map. With the first team competing successfully in division one and the 'A' team in division six, the committee began to discuss the future direction for the club. Ian Oxley and Phil Caplan, the media officer for the Rugby League Conference (RLC), had discussed the possibility of Rotherham joining the Conference. The RLC was, at the time, the leading summer competition for clubs based outside the traditional rugby league areas, and was seen as a potential breeding ground for future professional clubs. If an application to join the Conference was successful it could give the club a massive boost. The RLC had a national profile and received much more coverage in the rugby league media than the Pennine League did. The club hoped that adding a summer team to the already successful winter operation could help to attract new players, supporters and sponsors. The plan was for the new summer team to play matches at Herringthorpe Stadium, while the winter teams would continue to operate as they were in the Pennine League, playing matches at Oakwood School.

Herringthorpe Stadium

Darryl got involved in the discussions and a successful application to the RLC was made, and so in 2000 Rotherham Rugby League Club began gearing up for its first summer season. Unfortunately, because of a clash with athletics events, Herringthorpe Stadium wasn't available for the 2000 season. This setback seemed to have stopped the plan to join the Conference in its tracks until the Advertiser got involved. Following support from the newspaper, the Council agreed to mark out a pitch on Herringthorpe Playing Fields and rope it off for home games.

Despite being unable to use the stadium, the first season in the Rugby League Conference was a huge success, possibly the most successful in the history of the club. The Rugby Football League encouraged a number of Super League clubs to adopt Rugby League Conference clubs and support their development. I was working for Huddersfield Giants at the time and so I contacted Darryl to suggest that the Giants could support the Rotherham summer team. We quickly agreed a deal, the team would be called Rotherham Giants and Huddersfield would provide a playing kit, subsidised training gear and some off-field support. Jon Sharp, at the time Huddersfield's assistant coach, came to Rotherham to take a training session and a pre-season match between the clubs was planned for the beginning of the 2001 season

The club was going to be playing in a National competition and that helped Darryl to attract a number of new sponsors, including the Rotherham Advertiser.

We're putting our shirt on the Giants!

RUGBY LEAGUE

THE *Advertiser* will again be backing go-ahead Rotherham Giants all the way in this year's Rugby League Conference—so much so we're even putting our shirts on 'em!

After last year's successful link-up we're delighted to be involved with the Herringthorpe Stadium club for a second season, as the Giants look to go one better than last year's runner-up spot following their defeat in the Grand Final against Crawley Jets.

As a result our name will appear on the shirts of both the Rotherham first team squad and also the Junior Giants youth team.

It's the latest slice of good news for the ambitious club, who have already secured match sponsorship for each home game.

Said Giants head coach Darryl Osborne: "It's the first time we have tried to find match sponsors and we've been overwhelmed by the level of support for amateur rugby league in the area.

"It means we can finance the added demands of playing in a national competition and hopefully we will be able to repay our backers by going all the way in the Conference," he added.

Tickets for the showpiece opener against Huddersfield Giants on April 10 are now on general sale, with a bumper crowd expected. The cost is just £1 in advance (£2 pay on the night) while children will be admitted free of charge.

They can be obtained from the *Advertiser*'s Wellgate office, the Masons Arms at Wellgate, Philip Howard Books on Church Street or Herringthorpe Leisure Centre.

Meanwhile, Rotherham's Pennine League team face a toughie tomorrow, when they take on top of the table Siddall.

They were heavily beaten when the teams first met in September with Rotherham determined to prove a point. Kick off at Oakwood is 2.30pm.

The A team is away to Crigglestone A.

● Advertiser *Sports Editor Paul Rickett and Giants Head Coach Darryl Osborne.*

The income from the new sponsors meant the club could provide coaches to all the away games, additional training kit and quality physio support. They also received excellent coverage in the sports pages of the Advertiser. With the move to summer, rugby league in Rotherham was able to achieve a media profile locally that wasn't possible in the winter. With only cricket to compete with, the Advertiser published detailed match reports, photographs and previews and rugby league often featured on the back page, which in winter usually only contained Rotherham United's news.

The RLC in 2000 was organised into a number of regional leagues where clubs played ten fixtures against locally grouped teams, with the top two progressing from the regional league structure through to the knockout stages. Rotherham finished the regular season in second place in the Northern Division and so earned a play-off clash away to Birmingham Bulldogs, the Western Division champions. In a nail-biting encounter the Giants edged home by 29 points to 27

Shaun Rutherforth

In the play-off semi-final, held at Wilderspool before a Warrington versus Salford Super League game and 8,000 spectators, Rotherham beat Coventry Bears, a club that is now playing in the professional League One competition. As a result, Rotherham Giants made the Conference Grand Final in their first season. In the final they would face Crawley Jets at Coundon Road in Coventry.

The club organised two coaches for supporters and sponsors and had no trouble in filling both. Over the years Rotherham had taken part in (and won) a number of local cup finals, but this game had a much higher profile. It was the Grand Final of a National rugby league competition that involved clubs from all across England.

Unfortunately, on the day the Crawley team proved too strong and won by 38 points to 22 in front of a crowd of 635.

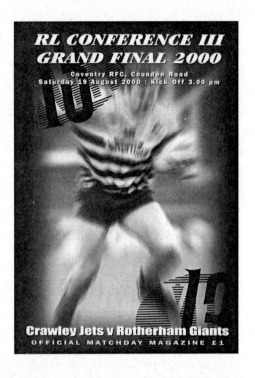

RL CONFERENCE III GRAND FINAL 2000

Coventry RFC, Coundon Road
Saturday 19 August 2000 : Kick Off 3.00 pm

Crawley Jets v Rotherham Giants
OFFICIAL MATCHDAY MAGAZINE £1

Pre-match formalities

IT was a bridge too far for the Rotherham Giants to cross when their great Conference adventure came to an end without the fairy tale finish everyone was hoping for.

They were beaten by Crawley Jets in a game which was a fine advert for the amateur rugby league.

Giants went into the game in confident mood after being the quiet achievers throughout the season and they made slight changes to the semi final line up bringing back forward Dan Lynch and the experienced Paul Scott was on the substitutes' bench.

Nigel Short was added to bring his experience and Richard Skidmore moved into the second row to replace the absent Rob North.

Rotherham's preparation had been superb and with a large travelling support they were looking forward to a big day out but coach Darryl Osborne warned his team that the Jets would be out of their blocks quickly.

Batty was nominated as man of the match although Weston, Moore and Nicky Colley all did well while Woolley and Lynch were commended for all their hard work.

Nevertheless, Osborne was left in an optimistic mood for the future and he said: "It has been a fantastic first summer season and all the people who have been involved deserve praise.

"The bulk of the players have come straight from a strenuous winter season and for them to perform in such a way has been amazing. I would like to thank all the coaching staff for their support and the Conference is now a major part of this country's rugby league with its fine organisation.

"We are proud to have been part of this although the end was heart breaking. But we have exceeded our wildest pre-season dreams."

Chairman Peter Moore added: "It has been hard work for us but I'm sure that next year with more time for preparation, we will be even more of a force."

Giants: Dean Jackson, Jasinski, Colley, Batty, Walker, Weston, Moore, Chadwick, Woolley, Archer, Skidmore, Darryl Jackson. Subs: Short, Lynch, Scott, Walls.

Highlights of the Grand Final were shown on the Sky Sports weekly rugby league magazine show 'Boots 'n' All', and the match report also featured prominently in League Express and League Weekly, two popular rugby league newspapers. Taking part in a National final and the coverage the club received in the Advertiser, the rugby league media and on Sky Sports had further raised the status and profile of rugby league in Rotherham. The expectation was that the club would be able to build on the successful first season and go on to win the Grand Final in 2001, while the successes of the summer were also expected to provide a boost to the winter team's fortunes in the Pennine League.

Chapter 7

Giants and Roosters

The new winter season began with a great deal of optimism. The first team, which remained in the Pennine League, was able to field a number of new recruits who had joined in the summer and as a result was very competitive in division one. The team was winning regularly and after a good first half of the season another promotion couldn't be ruled out. The influx of new players also boosted the 'A' team that was playing in Pennine division six. It was therefore understandable that there was some friction between the winter and summer teams when, in January 2001, the Giants began pre-season training for their second season in the RLC. There were some players at the club who just played for one of the teams but there were also quite a number who played both winter and summer. It was the players who were playing all year round who obviously struggled with the demands of combining matches in the Pennine League with a RLC pre-season training programme in January and February. The success of the summer team in 2000 had raised expectations so it wasn't surprising that the players who had been involved wanted to play again in 2001, but reconciling the demands of winter rugby with, at the same time, two nights a week of pre-season training was going to be very difficult.

However, despite the training issues, off the field the club was gearing up for what everyone hoped would be another successful summer season. The pre-season match between a Huddersfield Giants XIII and Rotherham Giants was arranged for Tuesday 10th April 2001 at Herringthorpe Stadium. The event was a big success, attracting a crowd of over 600. This was the biggest attendance ever for an amateur game in Rotherham. The Huddersfield Giants team was made up of trialists and Chris Roberts, the rugby league writer for the Huddersfield Examiner. Chris wrote an article for the Examiner describing his experience in Giants colours. Rotherham won the game 28-20, a result that gave the players a big boost going into the new season. Some of the new players Darryl had recruited must have believed that they were joining a club that was going to win the competition. The main aims of the pre-season game had been to increase the spectator base and further raise the profile of rugby league in Rotherham, and those aims were certainly achieved.

Unfortunately the 2001 season was not as successful as 2000. The Giants finished top of the Northern Division but only reached the quarter-finals of the RLC play-offs, losing narrowly to Coventry Bears by 28 points to 21. The profile of the club had been raised by its appearance in the 2000 Grand Final and the pre-season friendly win against Huddersfield, and only reaching the quarter-final was, I am sure, seen by some as a failure. That perceived lack of success may have added further to the tensions between the summer and winter teams that had begun in pre-season and couldn't really be adequately addressed. Players who wanted to play both winter and summer were always going to find it difficult to fit winter training and playing in with the summer pre-season programme in January and February. Unless players committed to playing for only one team there probably wasn't any way the problem was going to be resolved. The problems caused by the training issues were then added to when the club also began to fracture off the field. This was a similar situation to the events in 1990 when the Rangers first team had moved to Rotherham Cricket Club. The Giants were now using the Comrades Club in Wickersley for after match refreshments, while the two winter teams had moved from the Belvedere and were now based at the Masons Arms, a pub near the town centre.

In 2001/02 the winter team was still competing in Pennine League division one but the back to back promotions and progression of the 1990s hadn't continued. After a promising start, the season tailed off and Rotherham finished in mid-table for the second successive year.

Was the relative lack of success the first team had in division one, after starting the season well, caused by the training issues in January and February and fixture clashes when the Giants began playing pre-season friendlies?

The 2002 Giants

Another major problem arose at the beginning of 2002 when some key people on the committee began to lose interest. Ian Oxley, one of the founders of the Rotherham Rams and someone who had become heavily involved in all aspects of the merged club decided to leave. This was a big blow as the success of Rotherham Rugby League Club in the late 1990s was built on the number of people willing to contribute in off-field roles. Ian had been pivotal to that success and was impossible to replace. Darryl was also struggling, after the less successful second season, to find winter players willing to play in the summer. The club was financially sound, mainly because the high profile of the Giants made it much easier to attract new sponsors, but there weren't sufficient people willing to help off the field. The hope for 2002 was that despite the friction and loss of key administrators, once the winter season

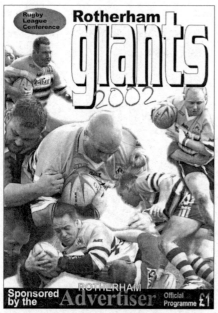

Launching the 2002 Giants

ended players would return to the summer team, new support staff would emerge and the Giants would have a good season.

The new summer season began on a positive note, helped by the celebration of twenty-five years of rugby league in Rotherham that was held at the Giants match against Chester Wolves on 11th May. The Giants lost the game by 24 points to 22 but that didn't spoil the event, attended by a number of players who had played in 1977.

Twenty five years of rugby league

To the casual observer the club was well established. The winter and summer teams had both been successful and the strength of the club appeared to be confirmed by its ability to turn out a second team in winter. I am sure that I wasn't the only player who had been involved in the first season who was impressed by the progress the club had made. In the early years, when we often played league fixtures with less than a full team, it would have been impossible to predict that the club would still be in existence twenty five years later. Unfortunately, a few weeks after the twenty-five year celebrations the Giants failed to raise a team and had to concede a fixture. I am sure that in 1977 we would have played the game with less than a full team and then re-grouped for the next fixture, but expectations had changed. The club was operating at a much higher level and perhaps in the minds of the players it was winning rather than fulfilling a fixture that was most important. The success of the club and the professional way in which games were approached meant that if the team was struggling for numbers then perhaps players who might have been prepared to play were not so keen if they thought they were likely to be on the losing side.

Following the conceded game an emergency meeting to decide the way forward was held at the Masons Arms. After what has been described as a fairly acrimonious discussion a vote was taken and the decision was that the club would, in the future, focus all its efforts and resources on winter rugby. Darryl Osborne felt that this was a backward step for rugby league in Rotherham and decided that he would leave. Darryl believed that the success of the RLC team had put rugby league in Rotherham on the map and that to continue to only play in a regional winter competition wasn't going give the club the profile it had achieved through playing in the Conference. The Giants conceded the majority of the rest of their games in the 2002 season. The RLC records show only three wins from their ten scheduled fixtures.

The winter teams renamed the Roosters began gearing up for the 2002/2003 season very optimistic about the future now that the club's main focus was back on winter rugby.

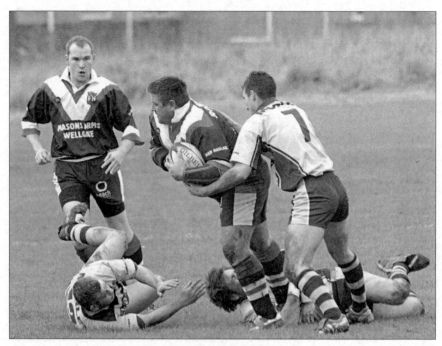

Darryl Jackson

The optimism was short lived as the Roosters first team had a very poor 2002/03 season. They struggled to compete in division one and after Christmas a string of defeats led to the team being relegated. The first time a Rotherham rugby league team had ever been relegated.

Surprisingly, after the club committee and players had taken the decision to concentrate on winter, the Giants summer team re-appeared in the Rugby League Conference in 2003. Maybe the disappointing winter season encouraged some of the winter players to continue playing in summer in the hope of achieving some success. Dave Williams, the former Maltby player, had taken over as Head Coach and his leadership and enthusiasm brought the club some early season success when, despite all the problems in 2002, they reached the final of the pre-season cup competition. The cup final was held at Penarth in South Wales, and the Giants were very disappointed to lose to a London Skolars team that contained a number of professional players. It could be argued that reaching that final didn't give the summer team the boost it hoped for and in fact losing to London Skolars started a slow decline. The Giants finished the league season in a disappointing fourth place in the North Midlands Division. However, the RLC had created a Shield competition and by finishing fourth the Giants qualified to take part in the Shield play-offs, where a number of creditable play-off performances saw the club reach the semi–final. What, after a good start, had been a fairly poor season managed to at least end on a positive note

The Roosters were still able to field two teams in the Pennine League but despite playing in a lower division, the first team continued to struggle and 2003/04 was another disappointing season. In 2004, on the other hand, the Giants fared much better in the RLC, ending the league campaign in the North Midlands Division in first place with nine wins from ten games. Despite the good league season they didn't make any progress in the play-offs, losing to Nottingham Outlaws in the first round. It is interesting to speculate on the reasons for the more successful 2004 season. Had two disappointing winter seasons encouraged the players to chase some success by playing in the summer?

In 2005 the Giants had another good league campaign and again reached the play-offs, but, for the second year running, they got no further than the first round. The success of the first year of summer rugby in 2000 was proving very hard to emulate. Ian Daintith, a former St Helens player who had moved to South Yorkshire, was working with Dave Williams and a number of new players joined the club but unfortunately the majority of the new recruits were not local, some coming from Wakefield and others from Doncaster. Rotherham had been successful in the late 1990s mainly because the team was made up of local players with a commitment to the club. The attempt to build a winning summer team by importing players from outside Rotherham wasn't helping to create a strong club. Meanwhile the Roosters poor results continued and they began the 2004/05 season in division three of the Pennine League. The club was still managing to turn out two winter teams but the 'A' team was near the bottom of division six and struggling for players. Recruitment without any junior teams was proving much more difficult and player morale was very low. The following winter season the Roosters only fielded one team. Many of the new recruits from Doncaster and Wakefield had left the club and with very few local players prepared to play in summer the Giants had to withdraw from the Rugby League Conference. Rugby league in Rotherham had reached a low point, one not seen since the early 1990s.

In 2005, much like in 1991, the winter team was left to pick up the pieces and the club made yet another move of home ground when they left Oakwood School and moved to Wickersley School, where they continued to play fixtures in division three of the Pennine League.

Rotherham Roosters

The Roosters still had a very big forward pack including, on occasions, stalwarts like Mick Haigh who had been with the club since the 1980s. After a season of consolidation it appeared that the Roosters might have turned a corner in 2006/07 and perhaps the 'good times' were on the way back. Craig Weston, who had played in Howard Charlesworth's under 17s team in 1988 and then in the open-age teams' right through the 1990s, had taken his coaching badges and took over as coach of the Roosters, having previously worked with the Sheffield Eagles junior teams. He recruited another former under 17 player Adam Charlesworth to help with pre-season training.

After he left Hull Kingston Rovers, Adam had played National Conference League (NCL) rugby for Hull Dockers and his conditioning skills and Craig's coaching ability had a dramatic impact on a team that began the season with a ten match unbeaten run. Despite having retired from rugby league six years earlier, Adam played a number of games for the Roosters, his experience on the field proving invaluable. Adam also persuaded his younger brother Evan to return to the club. Evan, after he left Wakefield Trinity Colts, had played open age rugby league mainly for Crigglestone All Blacks

Craig Weston

and his wealth of rugby league experience was an important factor in the great start to the season.

2007 Cup Winners

For most of 2006/07 the Roosters were top of the league and looked 'odds on' to gain promotion back to division two. It also seemed very likely that they would finish the season in top spot until Wyke, the club in second place, started to win all their games in hand. The final game of the season was between the two clubs and the winners would be crowned division three champions. Unfortunately the end of the season and the beginning of what could have been a new successful era for the club was marred by the news that Craig Weston, who was certainly the driving force behind the revival, was going to live and work in Australia. Wyke won the final league game very easily. Whether the players were demoralised by the news of Craig's departure or the fact that Wyke possibly fielded a number of 'ringers' isn't clear. However despite the heavy defeat the Roosters finished in second place, and so were promoted to division two.

After the progress of the previous season and the optimism generated the 2007/08 season began very badly. A disastrous opening home game against local rivals Dearne Valley Bulldogs saw the Roosters, with only eleven players, lose heavily. After that defeat the season continued to go downhill rapidly. Despite fielding a weakened team the Roosters were competitive in most of the games but couldn't manage to go on and win, and so by the middle of November the club was firmly anchored at the bottom of the league, having played and lost seven league games and also conceded one when they couldn't raise a team. After so many defeats morale was very low and possibly the final straw was losing by 56 points to 4 to Boothtown Terriers, the club next to bottom of division two. A couple of weeks after that game the club withdrew from the Pennine League and so, thirty years and seven months after Rotherham Rangers had been formed, rugby league disappeared completely from the sporting scene in the town.

Chapter 8

Re-Launch and Extinction

The end of winter rugby in Rotherham, after such a successful
2006/07 season, would probably have come as a surprise to an
outside observer. A club that achieves promotion and then folds less
than three months into the new season isn't a usual occurrence but there
were a number of factors which conspired to create the situation. The
loss of Craig Weston was probably the most important but added to that
the club also lost a number of key players who decided to retire over the
summer. Then towards the end of pre-season training Rob North, who
had taken over from Craig as coach, resigned. Andrew Tyers returned to
coach the team but some of the players who had got used to winning in
2006/07 were obviously not happy about playing in a losing team and
so numbers and interest dwindled, and in November 2007 it looked as
if anybody who lived in Rotherham and wanted to play rugby league
would need to look elsewhere for the first time in three decades

The club had probably remained in existence much longer than
anybody involved in the first season could ever have imagined. For
many other clubs in similar situations, ten or twelve seasons is usually
the maximum lifespan. Clubs often continue to function while ever the
enthusiasts involved in forming them are able to play. Rugby league in
Rotherham had managed to survive for over thirty years because in 1991,
when Rangers had looked like folding, Darryl Osborne, Kevan Cadman
and a group of enthusiastic players had kept it going. They were then
able to re-launch the club following the merger with Rotherham Rams.
A re-launch in 2008 was going to be different; the club had folded and

Rotherham Giants 2008

withdrawn from the League altogether, but fortunately there was still a small core group of interested players so it wasn't quite like starting from scratch. The group that met at the Masons Arms in December 2007 had to decide whether there was a future for rugby league in Rotherham and, if there was, whether the club should play in winter or summer. After a long discussion the decision was taken to re-launch as Rotherham Giants

John Dudley

and return to the Rugby League Conference. A big boost for the 2008 Giants was the return of Craig Weston, who moved back to Rotherham as his family had found it difficult to settle in Australia. Craig's involvement encouraged many of the old players to return with renewed enthusiasm. A new committee was voted in that would re-launch the club as Rotherham Giants and the players began gearing up for the new season playing home games at Herringthorpe Stadium.

Preparations for the season went very well; the Giants entered and won a pre-season nine-a-side competition held at Scunthorpe Rugby Union Club. The victory in the nines was the beginning of a good league season. John Dudley, a former first team regular at Rotherham Rugby Union Club and a legend in local rugby circles, had played with distinction for the Giants in earlier seasons and his return further boosted the club.

The Giants played some excellent rugby during the league campaign. They built on the nines win, fielded a big powerful team, and won most of their league games. Unfortunately, the success didn't continue when the team reached the end of season knockout phase. However, despite an early exit from the play-offs the 2008 season had been more successful than the enthusiasts who re-launched the club might have hoped for.

Preparations for the 2009 season began in January with over fifty players training regularly at the Phoenix Sports Club in Brinsworth. The number of new recruits from Hillsborough Hawks, Sheffield Forgers

Rob North

and local rugby union clubs meant that the Giants were able to enter a second team in the regional Merit League competition. There was a real optimism that perhaps the 2008 re-launch had begun a revival that the Giants could build on 2009.

'Burly' Mick Haigh still in action in 2009

Another boost came in early 2009 when a strong link was forged with Rotherham Rugby Union Club which meant that the Giants, who were still intending to play fixtures at Herringthorpe Stadium, were

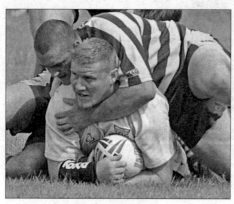

Gary Woodcock

able to use the clubhouse on Clifton Lane for after-match hospitality. How attitudes had changed! Very different to the late 1970s when Dave Platts had been threatened with a ban from the clubhouse if he continued to play rugby league. Chris Bell, the club Chairman, was planning to organise a junior section and Evan

Charlesworth, who was Vice Chairman, was successful in obtaining a Sport England Grant to support Chris's work.

The club seemed to be on the brink of really becoming established again when issues arose concerning team selection that started to have a negative impact. In an attempt to boost its on-field strength, the club drafted in a number of players from established winter clubs in West Yorkshire, obviously with the intention of winning every game. The incumbent first team players were not really affected but some of the new local players who had joined the club in the close season quickly became disillusioned at the lack of first team opportunities. Unfortunately, regardless of how well they played in the Merit League very few of these young men got an opportunity to prove themselves in the first team mainly due to the large number of 'outsiders' that were brought in for every match.

The first team had a good season on the field but didn't make any progress in the play-offs, and at the end of August many of the young players who had joined in pre-season left the club and didn't return the

Steve Burns

following year. The positive re-launch in January 2008 had by the end of 2009 turned into the beginning of a slow decline.

In 2010 and 2011 the Giants team was often bolstered by players from out of the area. Craig Weston had gone back to Australia and things looked pretty bleak, Dave Williams returned to coach the team but recruiting and retaining players was now becoming the major issue. There was a great reliance on players from Wakefield and Sheffield, and with only one team and very few local players it was getting increasingly difficult to see a positive future for rugby league in Rotherham.

2010 Giants

The 2010 Giants, after a good league season, had to concede their first round play-off game at East Leeds. This followed a disagreement over the kick off time which left the Giants unable to field a full team. The disappointing end to the season was perhaps a sign of things to come.

Chris Bell had taken on much of the administration and he was finding it very difficult to persuade new players to join. The fact that it was costing over £200 to stage a home game at Herringthorpe Stadium only added to the problems. In 2011, when the Giants finished next to bottom of the RLCs Yorkshire East Division with only three wins, it looked very likely that without a dramatic influx of new players and a reduction in match costs the club was going to find it impossible to continue.

In September 2011 the sport of rugby league was re-organised at Community level and a new league, the Yorkshire Men's League, was formed to replace the RLC in Yorkshire. Rotherham, reverting to their old 'Roosters' name, joined the new Yorkshire Men's League and made one last move

Action from the 2012 season

in an attempt to revive interest. They decided to play home games at Dinnington Rugby Union Club, almost 10 miles from Herringthorpe Stadium and Rotherham town centre, hoping that the move would attract some new recruits and also reduce match costs. The 2012 team was made up of a few former Roosters and Giants and a number of rugby union players that Gary Woodcock had recruited from Retford, but the expected recruits from Dinnington never materialised and unfortunately, mainly because of a lack of numbers, the club finally folded.

Ironically both Darryl Osborne and I attended one of the final home games in May 2012. The opposition was local rivals Hillsborough Hawks, whose team contained a number of former Rotherham players. The game wasn't completed due to an injury to the referee, but at the point when the game was abandoned Rotherham were losing. The club played just four games in 2012, folding after their final game at Leeds Akkies on Saturday 16th June, ironically a game they managed to win by 24 points to 18. The win didn't boost morale and Chris Bell, who had worked very hard to keep the club going, decided that with so few committed players the club wouldn't be able to complete the season.

Apart from the two months in 2007 after the Roosters had folded and before the Giants re-formed, there had been a rugby league club in Rotherham for thirty-five years. The demise of the Roosters in 2012 finally saw the end of rugby league in Rotherham.

One of the last Rotherham teams

Chapter 9

What Went Wrong?

In 2016, anyone from Rotherham who wants to play rugby league would have to travel to Doncaster or Sheffield to find their nearest club, a similar situation to that which existed in the 1970s. There have been amateur rugby league clubs in Doncaster since the 1920s and, although many have folded, changed their name or re-located, the game has continued to be played in a town that is very similar in many ways to Rotherham. It would be easy to argue that the reason there are still amateur rugby league clubs in Doncaster is because the town has a professional club. However, since its formation in 1951 Doncaster Rugby League Club has usually struggled both on the field and in its ability to attract supporters. The club has had short periods of success but that success has never really been sustained for more than a season or two. There is a hard-core of rugby league fans in Doncaster but the professional club hasn't the profile and winning record that would attract newcomers to the game in any large quantity. The professional club had a dreadful 2015 season while the two amateur clubs in the town are both well established and thriving.

The absence of a professional club may have explained the relative lack of public knowledge of rugby league in Rotherham in the 1970s. However, despite there being no professional club, rugby league did at times have a high profile, and for several seasons the club appeared to have become firmly established.

The important question is why, after appearing to become established and successful, has rugby league disappeared from the sporting scene in Rotherham?

In 1977 I had no long term ambitions for the club apart from some sort of vague hope that there would be an opportunity to play rugby league in Rotherham for as long as I was able to carry on playing. Towards the end of my time with the club, and after I retired from playing, I did have hopes that we could establish a permanent presence for rugby league in the town, find a ground that we would remain at for more than a few years and perhaps apply to join the amateur game's flagship competition the National Conference League (NCL). However, I didn't have any real idea of how we were going to achieve those objectives, possibly one of the reasons that I decided to sever my connections with Rotherham Rangers in 1991. I couldn't see the way forward and I didn't really believe that anyone else involved at the time could either. I was wrong about that as Darryl Osborne proved during the 1990s

The re-birth that followed the first team folding in 1991 and then the subsequent revival, merger with Rotherham Rams and the formation of the summer team couldn't have happened when I left the club in 1991, so I think I probably took the right decision in leaving when I did. The people who took the club on, particularly Darryl, certainly knew what they thought was the best way forward. The revival in fortunes, the junior teams and the formation of the summer team gave the club a great platform not only to become established in Rotherham, but also a real opportunity to develop into a club capable of competing with the best in amateur rugby league. An ideal destination would've been the National Conference League. The NCL has four divisions that contain all the leading amateur clubs in the country and there are minimum standards that clubs have to achieve in order to join the league. The clubs in the NCL attract the best amateur players and the standard of rugby was far superior to that played by clubs in the Rugby League Conference. In 2000, because the NCL was a winter competition there was no obvious route for clubs to progress from the RLC to the NCL. However, now that the NCL has moved to play in the summer then a summer club as strong as Rotherham was in 2000, providing it had a junior structure, could, in 2016, have made a successful application to join the NCL. Whether playing regular fixtures against the top amateur clubs could have been sustained is another matter. The standard of rugby in the NCL and the quality of the opposition means the challenge for clubs outside the established areas is that of playing a tough game every week, recruiting players who can play at that level and remaining competitive. Darryl had taken the club to new heights in 2000 and because it proved impossible to replicate that achievement in the seasons that followed perhaps a Rotherham club reaching the higher echelons of amateur rugby league was just a 'pipe dream'.

The players turning out for Rotherham in the late 1990s had got used to winning regularly and reaching cup finals. It does seem that the 2000 season when the club reached the RLC Grand Final was an achievement that every subsequent summer campaign had to try to emulate. Anything less than an appearance in the RLC Grand Final appeared to be seen as failure. The junior set up, which in the late 1990s had produced young players capable of making the transition into the first team, was struggling from 2000 onwards. The lack of juniors feeding into the open age teams meant that it was even more important that young local players continued to be recruited in order to ensure the future of the club. The recruitment opportunities that existed in the 1980s and 1990s were still there; young players from the Rotherham area playing junior rugby league in Sheffield and students leaving Sheffield Hallam and Sheffield University should have been recruitment targets, but it seems that chasing short-term success rather than recruiting and encouraging young local players became the priority, a priority that, in my view, contributed to the demise of the club.

I can understand why the players involved with the club in 2002 decided that they preferred to focus all their efforts on the winter team. They joined the club to play rugby league and their main concern was to be part of an enjoyable experience on a Saturday which, at the time, the Roosters provided. The games in the Pennine League were competitive and prior to 2002 there were more wins than losses. You didn't have to travel too far for an away match and you got the opportunity to have a few pints with your mates after the game. The problems came when the team wasn't winning regularly and some of the better players moved on or retired. Recruiting new players who are capable of stepping into a team that is playing at a level that players new to rugby league would struggle with becomes a problem, as it had in the 1980s. When the club started, new players with limited rugby experience could cope because the club was operating at a very low standard, one that inexperienced players could handle. That certainly wasn't the case in the 2000s and, once the decline began, apart from bringing in players from outside the town who had little long-term commitment to the club there wasn't very much that could be done to halt it. In areas where rugby league is established, finding new experienced players isn't too difficult. If a team folds in Wakefield or Castleford the players will just move down the road to another amateur club or a new club will be formed at a different pub. Towns like Rotherham outside established rugby league areas present a different set of problems. Finding players in Rotherham capable of stepping into a team that is playing in the top divisions of the summer competition or division one of the Pennine League is very difficult.

It is easy, as an observer, to criticise the decision to import so many outsiders and I am not sure that I would have taken a different decision given the situation the club was in. The Giants were playing at Herringthorpe Stadium, the Rotherham Advertiser was giving the club excellent coverage and there was obviously a burning desire to emulate the exploits of the 2000 Giants. The problem for the club was that when immediate success didn't come then the players from out of town became disillusioned. They didn't want to travel long distances to be involved with a losing team. When the 'out of town' players left there was nobody with experience to replace them.

The other major problem the club had in establishing rugby league in Rotherham was the lack of a permanent home ground. Between 1977 and 2012 the club used nine different home grounds and more than a dozen pubs or clubs as their base. Had the club stayed at Pitches Sports Club then perhaps the junior structure would have remained in place and the player recruitment problems may not have arisen. I know that in some cases the decision to move grounds was forced on the club but some of the other moves were not. If the club hadn't moved around so much would it have survived? I am pretty sure that if the club had remained at Pitches it would still be in existence. Rugby union clubs and some amateur rugby league clubs with their own clubhouses and facilities provide a focal point both for the community and for ex-players to remain involved. Of the hundreds of players who played rugby league in Rotherham, very few took up off-field roles after they retired from playing. Returning to watch games at the ground where you played might have encouraged some former players to stay involved. The club would have been much stronger if more ex-players had remained as active members adding their experience to that of people like Darryl Osborne, Kevan Cadman, Steven Beech, Andrew Tyers and Chris Bell, all of whom either stayed with the club or returned to take up an off-field role.

All the people involved both on and off the field wanted the club to be successful but chasing success doesn't necessarily ensure a club becomes firmly established. A continuous supply of local players and a permanent base does make a massive difference. Rugby league, like all team sports, is about winning and losing but only one of the two teams playing a game can win. If you join a rugby league club expecting to always play in a winning team then you are in for some disappointing experiences. Anyone involved in amateur sport has to recognise that there will be good and bad days, but because you are playing for fun the memories and the friends you make are what matters. Sport is a big part of many people's lives and it is such a shame that after thirty-five years the opportunity to play rugby league is no longer available in Rotherham.

Conclusion

In chapter nine I gave my views on what caused the demise of rugby league in Rotherham. If you played rugby league for the Rangers, Roosters or Giants you may, of course, disagree with my views and if you do have an alternative opinion about what went wrong I would be very happy to hear it. There isn't any sort of template or formula for organising an amateur club in 'alien' territory. Everyone involved with organising that type of club makes decisions that at the time seem the correct ones but can have unintended consequences. Organising an amateur club is a very time consuming hobby, one that becomes a major part of your life. I enjoyed most of my involvement with rugby league in Rotherham as I hope is clear when you read the book. I have some good memories and made some good friends. However, I am pretty sure that some of the mistakes I made contributed to the eventual outcome. The aim of this book isn't to blame anybody for what went wrong, rather to tell the story. I hope that perhaps the story of rugby league in Rotherham might be seen as a 'cautionary tale' for anyone involved in organising an amateur rugby league club. The mistakes made and some of the decisions taken over the years certainly contributed to what happened in 2012 but there were other major issues that arose that nobody at the club could control. Those issues were injuries to senior players, key players retiring, administrators and coaches leaving, terrible fixture planning and grounds becoming too costly or unavailable. The impact of those events, which nobody had any real control over, must have also contributed to the final outcome.

It isn't a disaster that rugby league is no longer played in Rotherham. The town has many social and economic problems and a thriving amateur rugby league club isn't going to resolve any of those. The hundreds of people who played for the Rangers, Roosters and Giants are, in my opinion, very fortunate that they were involved in the sport of rugby league. I am sure that because of their involvement they have made many friends and have memories that will stay with them for the rest of the lives.

Other Titles Published by Dropkick Books

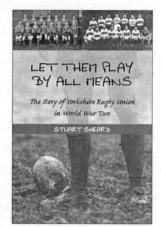
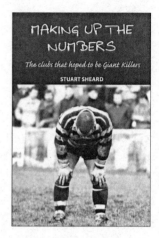

Available from www.ypdbooks.com